As someone who has coached thousands of kids and adults, Ross passionately talks about the power of carefully chosen words. He has had such an incredible impact on many students', teachers', and community members' lives, especially mine.

As a coach, minister, father, and grandfather, Ross's words in this book will change or enhance your life over and over again.

Jerry Korum, CEO, Korum Automotive Group

In *Winning Words*, Ross Hjelseth takes us beyond the quips to a coherent approach to life and leadership. Hjelseth's transparency and humility make the work compelling, and the stories from a lifetime of high-quality leadership remind us of the work we do person by person, day by day. This is an inspiring read, and one that undoubtedly can strengthen your ability to lead coherently and effectively.

Ms. Katie Wiens, Executive Director, Council on Educational Standards and Accountability

Do you desire to be a leader of influence? *Winning Words* will ignite your purpose to encourage and lift those around you.

Josh Dunn, President, PremierMedia Inc.

I'm so excited for this book to land in the hands of readers so its words can shape their lives as it has mine. Ross is a mentor, friend, and was a boss to me for more than a decade; as an author, he combines all of these. Truly he has been anointed by God. Allow God's wisdom through Ross's words and experience to bring you to another level of impact on your world.

Ms. Erin Francis, Pastor and Author

Ross Hjelseth has been a champion coach and a champion in the business world. And now he has brought together great champions to share with us how powerful WORDS are in driving our ability to WIN every day.

Ben Newman, Performance Coach for Alabama
Crimson Tide and Kansas State Wildcats

WINNING WORDS

Speaking Life
— to —
Influence Others

ROSS HJELSETH

WESTBOW
PRESS®
A DIVISION OF THOMAS NELSON
& ZONDERVAN

WestBow Press books may be ordered through booksellers or by contacting:

WestBow Press
A Division of Thomas Nelson & Zondervan
1663 Liberty Drive
Bloomington, IN 47403
www.westbowpress.com
1 (866) 928-1240

ISBN: 978-1-9736-9315-4 (sc)
ISBN: 978-1-9736-9314-7 (hc)
ISBN: 978-1-9736-9316-1 (e)

Library of Congress Control Number: 2020910581

Printed in United States of America.

WestBow Press rev. date: 07/13/2020

CONTENTS

Acknowledgments...vii
Introduction..ix

Faith...1
Training 16
Discipline..31
Motivation...44
Perseverance..62
Humor and Fun 78
Leadership 94
Relationships..112
Teamwork 133
Success...148
Character / Integrity / Legacy 167

Notes..179

ACKNOWLEDGMENTS

As I near the completion of this book, I want to recognize and thank the good Lord for the people who have given me the most help and encouragement along this journey.

First, and most importantly, I thank God for giving me life after two cancer surgeries in 2015. As I recovered from the second surgery, I spent time both reflecting and looking forward. During this time, I decided on twelve goals that I hoped to accomplish should I continue to live. One of those goals was to write a book, and now that goal has become a reality. You hold it in your hands.

When I think of key people who encouraged me on this journey, one of the first thoughts that comes to mind is Jim Wacker's direction in 1977 to create a notebook on motivation. That assignment was the starting line for a journey I am completing in 2020. Thanks, Coach, for the opportunity and direction.

Thank you to my good friend Doug Burton, owner of VSG Marketing, for his help with the research materials and tools that made the project attainable. His consistent "yes" was inspirational.

A big thanks to all the coaches and leaders who contributed the sayings at the end of each chapter. Winning words are spoken by key people every day to influence others. This book is a collection of those favorite expressions used over and over to make a difference in people. The most successful coaches and leaders are gifted communicators who choose their words well.

I want to thank Krysti Hall, who gave me direction, copyediting, and encouragement at every turn. I have learned that writing a book is not a one-person effort, but instead requires the expertise and experience of others. Krysti has given me that since the beginning.

A special note of appreciation to those who have endorsed this book. Each has shared his or her insights about the value proposition herein. I am hopeful that my readers agree with those who have spoken positively.

Much gratitude to my sons, who have consistently encouraged me to keep on keeping on with the project. They believed in their dad, and that put wind in my sails. Thanks, Brandon and Tyler.

And I am thankful to Ronni, my beautiful wife, for her continued faithful support and encouragement in all I do. Her "You can do it" and "It will be great" affirmations have come at just the right times. She has helped make this book a reality.

To my readers, please use the things you learn from this book to "speak life" into people around you each day. Yours may be the only encouragement they receive. You can do it! I hope and pray this book is a blessing to many, today and for future generations.

INTRODUCTION

Born on a farm in North Dakota, I grew up with a love for sports and great admiration for the coaches at my small high school of approximately 125 students.

From my first peewee baseball coach to my high school basketball coach, who had a dynamic influence on my life, I did my best to please and honor each of my coaches. They were my role models, and I set out to be like them—much to the chagrin of my father, who had hoped I would take over a successful farming operation.

As a student athlete, I listened closely to my coaches' words and repeated them to my teammates. In 1977, this desire to collect and pass along powerful words from coaches was enhanced by an assignment from Jim Wacker, who gave me the opportunity to become a graduate assistant coach on his football staff at North Dakota State University. Coach Wacker tasked me with creating a notebook on motivation for the Bison coaching staff. My summer was spent collecting a wealth of information, and I was pleased to hand a three-ring binder to each coach just before we began fall camp. The copy that remains on my shelf today was the foundation for the book you hold in your hand.

Moving into head coaching roles in high school and college football, I continued to collect motivational sayings for locker rooms and playbooks, and I put a lot of effort into preparing just the right pregame and halftime speeches for my teams. Over the years, I became a husband, a father to two boys, and, later, an education administrator. An avid learner, I constantly sought out effective words to apply and share in each of those contexts.

In November 2015, during a ten-day recovery from kidney cancer surgery, I identified twelve goals I wanted to accomplish. One of those goals was to write a book. After a thirty-five-year career in football coaching, as well as a lifetime in leadership roles, I renewed my focus on the power of people's words and the effect those words have on others. This work is the culmination of an effort that began in 1977 and continued over four decades.

I am a firm believer that we choose our words. When we choose them with care, they can be a blessing to others. This book is a compilation of words, sayings, and expressions used by successful coaches at every level of sports, as well as other leaders I have met during my career.

These sayings have been grouped into several areas of focus and accompanied by some of my own story and things that I've learned. I hope the words on these pages will have a positive effect on any reader, regardless of age, career, personality, or life situation. We are all affected by the power of others' words. At the right time, in the right circumstances, the right words can be powerful.

FAITH

- Complete trust or confidence in someone or something
- Strong belief in the doctrines of a religion based on spiritual conviction rather than proof
- A strongly held belief
- Synonyms: trust, belief, confidence, conviction, credence, reliance, dependence, optimism, hope, expectation; religion, church, sect, denomination, persuasion, belief, ideology, creed, teaching, dogma, doctrine

Because of my strong belief in God, it is important to me to begin this book with some words on the topic of faith. As a team member, coach, teacher, president of an organization, chairman of a board, head of a private school, and head of a household, I know and have experienced firsthand the value of faith in God, faith in leadership, faith in family members, faith in colleagues, and faith in teammates.

We invest our faith in many people and places each day, but I believe faith in God is the most important. God is my provider, Father, leader, and friend. From Him, I receive daily direction, inspiration, and wisdom. I also have strong confidence, based on several decades of life experience and the Bible's promises, that He guides my steps and facilitates good outcomes. According to Psalm 37:23, "The Lord directs the steps of the godly. He delights in every detail of their lives." Furthermore, Romans 8:28 tells us, "And we know that God causes everything to work together for the good of those who love God and are called according to his purpose for them."

FAITH AND DIRECTION

At a young age, I knew I wanted to be a coach. The people I looked up to the most, especially during my high school years, were my coaches. In particular, I wanted to be like my high school basketball coach, Ray Stinar, who also taught business education. When enrolling at Mayville State College, I chose to major in business education and physical education, with a primary focus on becoming a coach, as a result of Coach Stinar's influence.

Just three years after completing my bachelor's degree, I had the opportunity to become a graduate assistant football coach at North Dakota State University. After completing my graduate work, I was fortunate to spend seven seasons as a full-time assistant coach at NDSU. Those years coaching at NDSU were some of the greatest years of my life.

In 1985 I was hired as the head football coach for the University of Puget Sound in Tacoma, Washington. My wife, Ronni, and I moved from North Dakota to the Pacific Northwest, where we began attending a church known as Life Center. The senior pastor, Fulton Buntain, quickly became quite important to our family. A few years into our friendship, Pastor Buntain suggested I consider leaving the college football world to help expand the school that was a part of Life Center's ministry. The preschool that he had begun in 1974 had grown to include kindergarten through eighth grade. Fulton asked me to join the Life Christian School board, and I agreed to do so. During my time on the board, he continued to nudge me about accepting the task of adding a high school and solidifying the middle school. Although I declined for the better part of three years, Fulton kept up his campaign, and in 1992 God began softening my heart and helping me see the possibilities for my future in Christian education. In the fall of 1993, after many hours of prayer and consideration, I resigned from my position as head football coach of the Loggers after nine seasons.

Days later, I assumed oversight of Life Christian School and began work as the founding headmaster of Life Christian Academy, a yet-to-be-created college-preparatory school. Thus began my call to full-time ministry and a twenty-six-year tenure as headmaster of a school community that has been a significant blessing throughout two and a half decades of my life. (As a bonus, I was also LCA's head football coach for twelve years, so I didn't actually have to leave coaching!)

Sometimes faith means taking the step that is in front of you, not knowing where it will lead but confident that God wants you to take it. Our move from North Dakota to Washington, and the decision nine years later to leave college coaching, were steps of this kind.

At other times, faith is believing that the future we are hoping for and working toward is going to become real. Hebrews 11:1 describes faith as "the reality of what we hope for; it is the evidence of things we cannot see." We move forward in faith so that we can achieve a goal seen not with our eyes, but only in our minds. We work and pray every day, pressing on toward what we believe can become a reality. The stronger our faith, the stronger our ability to stay the course and persevere. Through the challenges that arise along the way, we can call upon our faith to help us overcome obstacles, mistakes, setbacks, and losses.

My pursuit of college coaching as a career, raising two sons with Ronni, and leading Life Christian Academy have all been parts of my faith journey. In each case, I knew God had assigned a clear mission, believed He would equip me and those He placed alongside me to accomplish it well, and did my best every day to fulfill the roles He had given me.

Two years before my departure from LCA, the academy's preschool, elementary, middle, and high schools were all recognized as the very best in the South Puget Sound region. What a high note on which to finish this season of Christian schooling! One faith step at a time, God led us into many opportunities, including raising our two sons within this school community and now watching our young grandchildren learn and grow as Life Christian Academy students.

FAITH AND FAMILY

Youth growing up in family homes experience varied levels of love and affection. In any setting at any time, if you were to survey people about their childhood experiences, the accounts and corresponding emotions would differ widely.

As a college coach, high school coach, and headmaster of a school that serves children from preschool through high school, I have encountered a broad spectrum of family structures, situations, relationships, and dynamics. I've also watched many of those children and youth become adults, spouses, and parents, which has taught me quite a bit about the effect their childhood homes have on the way they approach building their own homes and families.

For instance, I have seen that a lack of love or affection in childhood can cause a void in certain areas of mental health and well-being. Understandably, this often results in a lack of faith in family. Most of us probably know at least one person who has had to do some personal work as an adult to overcome the brokenness of an unhealthy relationship experienced in childhood.

Conversely, children who grow up in loving homes where they regularly hear words of encouragement and wisdom will likely develop strong faith in the family unit—a support system that is invaluable throughout life and meant to be perpetuated from generation to generation. Among the greatest gifts that husbands, wives, fathers, and mothers can pass along to their spouses or children are the gifts of faith in God and faith in family.

BUILDING FAITH

How do we obtain, attain, sustain, and grow faith?

Every one of us encounters daily opportunities to grow our faith simply by living life and engaging with all it encompasses. Whether joyful or challenging, each life situation presents an invitation to strengthen our awareness of God's provision and sustaining grace. Over time, our journeys become our testimony to God's faithfulness through all seasons and circumstances.

We can also build our faith through reading, listening, or observing acts of faith demonstrated by others. Building our faith depends in part upon continued learning from others. Pastors, priests, and other religious leaders are charged with being the teachers of their respective faiths. These spiritual leaders use words to teach, encourage, and lead people to grow in faith and faithfulness.

When I asked Tyler Sollie, the current senior pastor of Life Center in Tacoma, how he knows what to say regarding faith, he told me there isn't a cookie-cutter method. His direction often comes from having lived a particular concept or truth himself before speaking to his congregation about it. Personal conviction and experience are effective stimuli for shaping messages to share with others. Pastor Sollie also cultivates his own continuous learning on several levels, constantly weaving new knowledge and experiences into the fabric of his written and spoken messages to the people he leads.

A pastor may use different approaches to faith topics at different times. Sometimes, Pastor Sollie explained, circumstances in the world help determine what needs to be addressed to help people navigate well. He used the analogy of a shepherd being responsible for taking care of his flock of sheep. A pastor can use timely words to guide his "sheep" to a better place in a season of challenge or uncertainty. In this respect, the words chosen by a pastor are a gleaming example of the potential effect a thoughtful message spoken with passion can have on a group of people.

The most discerning spiritual leaders have a keen proficiency for saying just the right thing at just the right time. They use their words to affect and influence those they are leading.

TENACIOUS FAITH

By definition, faith is uninterrupted, although it may be weak at times.

In the summer of 2002, Jackie McLean, my sister-in-law and a single mother, moved with her two children from North Dakota to Tacoma, Washington. Before the move, Jackie had undergone a bilateral mastectomy for breast cancer, followed by a report from her doctors that all cancerous tissue had been removed. As she settled in Tacoma, she and her children were enjoying their new life in the Pacific Northwest, building a new level of relationship with nearby family members who had once lived far away.

Far too soon, we learned that Jackie's strength and faith were to be tested yet again. Just three months after arriving in the Pacific Northwest, she felt another lump. A consultation with her physician and subsequent testing revealed that the cancer had returned and spread to another area in her body. This shocking news devastated the entire family, but Jackie, ever the person of strong faith, reassured us that she would handle whatever was to come with dignity, grace, and strength.

Over the next weeks and months, our family walked with Jackie through tests, chemotherapy, and radiation treatments that left her fatigued and weak. As we struggled to sustain hope, Jackie remained a pillar of strength, and her faith in her heavenly Father's promise of joy with Him in heaven never wavered. Each day she clung more tightly to His promise of eternal life. We were all at her bedside on the day she passed, and typical of Jackie, she was completely at peace with God's plan for her life.

I will always remember Jackie's steadfast perseverance, genuine smile, and loving spirit. She was never bitter, but instead always resilient in her attitude and testimony to others. Although we all grieved her challenging disease and its pending outcome, Jackie was a continuous encourager and example of true faith, even in the valley of the shadow of death. She was living the promise of Isaiah 26:3: "You will keep in perfect peace all who trust in you, all whose thoughts are fixed on you!"

FAITH IN COLLEAGUES

In our workplaces and professional lives, most of us accomplish significantly more together than we do as individuals. We rely on our colleagues at work and even employees at other companies to do their part and go the distance. When everyone does what they have committed to do, we make collective progress toward goals that we couldn't accomplish alone.

You will read more about this dynamic in the chapters on relationship and teamwork, but it's worth noting here that faith in other people is a key component of success. When reaching for and achieving higher levels of success, faith in coworkers and colleagues is a significant contributing factor far more often than not. As an often-quoted African proverb says, "If you want to go fast, go alone. If you want to go far, go together."

FAITH AND HARDSHIP

Whether placed in God, ourselves or other people, or a process or principle, faith plays a key role in providing the strength and perseverance to "keep on keeping on" in difficult times.

We've all read or heard about situations in which people faced dire circumstances. Faced with life-threatening challenges, people must rely on robust faith—faith that they can endure or overcome, faith that good will prevail, faith that they will be rescued. Sometimes in the most difficult of settings, those who survived hours, days, weeks, and sometimes months did so because of their faith, which gave them uncommon hope.

Chaim Ferster was a Holocaust survivor who cheated death in eight Nazi concentration camps during World War II. During his two-year ordeal, he faced horrific labor conditions, malnutrition, and typhus before finally being freed by Allied forces at the very moment he and his fellow prisoners had been rounded up to be shot. During his time in captivity, Ferster endured outdoor work in temperatures well below freezing, group showers with ice-cold water, starvation, pneumonia, scenes of stacked bodies on pallets, and continuous abuse by German soldiers. Within a few days of his arrival at Auschwitz, he realized that the flames coming from four large chimneys belonged to the crematorium. And yet, despite hopeless conditions with most people around him dying, Chaim

Ferster continued to rely on faith and hope that he would survive. Against all odds, he did.[1]

FAITH AS A FRAMEWORK

In addition to Hebrews 11:1, a handful of Bible verses have spoken pointedly to me about the role of faith in a believer's life, including these three:

> And it is impossible to please God without faith. Anyone who wants to come to him must believe that God exists and that he rewards those who sincerely seek him. (Hebrews 11:6)

> Let us run with endurance the race God has set before us. We do this by keeping our eyes on Jesus, the champion who initiates and perfects our faith. (Hebrews 12:1b–2a)

> Because of Christ and our faith in him, we can now come boldly and confidently into God's presence. (Ephesians 3:12)

I recently came across "The Game Guy's Prayer," a clipping I had tucked away in my files years ago. To me, it exemplifies well how sincere faith can shape our outlook and approach to the "game" of life.

> Dear God: Help me to be a sport in this little game of life. I don't ask for an easy place in the lineup; play me anywhere You need me. I ask only for the stuff to give You 100 percent of what I've got. If all the hard drives seem to come my way, I thank You for the compliment. Help me to remember that You won't ever let anything come my way that You and

I can't handle. And help me to take the bad breaks as part of the game. Help me to understand that the game is full of knocks and knots and trouble, and make me thankful for them. Help me to get so that the harder they come, the better I like it.

And O God, help me to always play on the square. No matter what the other players do, help me to come clean. Help me to study the Book so that I'll know the rules, and to study and think a lot about the Greatest Player who ever lived and other players who are told about in the Book. If they found that the best part of the game was helping other guys who were out of luck, help me to find it out too. Help me to be a regular feller with the other players.

Finally, O God, if fate seems to uppercut me with both hands, and I'm laid on the shelf in sickness or old age or something, help me to take that as part of the game, too. Help me not to whimper or squeal that the game was a frame-up or that I had a raw deal.

When in the falling dusk I get the final bell, I ask for no lying complimentary stones. I'd only like to know that You feel that I've been a good game guy.[2]

I am a big believer that God gives each of us spiritual gifts that we are to use to serve Him and others. My personal mission statement is "to serve God and people to the best of my ability."

In 1977, my work on a motivation notebook resulted in a collection of sayings and poems, including a poem titled "The Gospel According to You." The word *gospel* means good news, and the first four books of the Bible's New Testament are referred to as the gospels.

Each gospel presents an account of the life of Jesus written from the unique perspective of one of His companions and closest friends.

In its eight short lines, "The Gospel According to You" poses the idea that each of us can live the gospel each day, which then becomes the gospel that other people see. I include it here as a reminder that none of us lives in a vacuum. Our lives and words have an effect on others, just as theirs influence us.

> You are writing a gospel,
> A chapter each day,
> By deeds that you do,
> By words that you say.
> Men read what you write,
> Whether faithless or true:
> Say! What is the gospel
> According to you?[3]

As I look back at my life—the leaders God placed in my life as I was growing up, the woman who became my wife, my experiences in college football, and the man who kept inviting me into an adventure in Christian education—I can see God's fingerprints in every season and place. I am a testimony to Hebrews 11:1. God has provided far beyond what I could have ever imagined, and each step of faith laid the foundation for the next. He knew the plans He had for my family and me.

SAYINGS

> *Commit to the Lord whatever you do, and your plans will succeed. (Proverbs 16:3)*
> —Vernon Fox, Faith Lutheran High School

> *I am only one, but I am one.*
> *I can't do everything, but I can do something.*
> *That which I can do, I ought to do.*
> —Edward Everett Hale

I know we're not all of the same religious persuasion. I think the Lord's Prayer ought to cover everyone.
—Ara Parseghian, University of Notre Dame

Think big, pray big, believe big, and you'll be big.
—Norman Vincent Peale

In all labor there is profit. (Proverbs 14:23)

Mongoo-up.
—Kent Nevin, Fife High School
  [Refers to a mongoose fighting a cobra]

As iron sharpens iron, so one man sharpens another. (Proverbs 27:17)
—Ken Rucker, University of Texas

Keep dreaming of championships!
—Larry Kindbom, Washington University

Every day is fourth and one.
—Erik Brown, Eldorado High School

Make your next step your best step; it might be a step to the end.
—Erik Brown, Eldorado High School

Never think you can overcome the easiest things, but always believe you can overcome the hardest things.
—Fran Schwenk, University of St. Mary

Lord, give us the faith to expect greater things. Whatever we do, let us give it our best, anxious in nothing and at peace with the promise that when we've done all we can, you'll take care of the rest.
—Kurt Keener, Gilbert Christian School

Do you not know that in a race all the runners compete, but only one receives the prize? So run that you may obtain it. (1 Corinthians 9:24)

As soon as you learn to trust yourself, you will learn to win.
—Johann Wolfgang von Goethe

If you know the enemy and know yourself, you need not fear the result of a hundred battles.
—Sun Tzu

Learn from—but forget—the last play. The next one is the most important.
—Bill Diedrick, high school and college coach

Faith, family, academics, football, social life.
—Chris Fisk, Central Washington University

Cast your bread upon the waters, and it will come back with strawberry jam.
—Donna Westering, Pacific Lutheran University

Make the least of what is gone and the most of what is ahead.
—Johnny Majors, University of Tennessee

Everyone should know the six things we do in the red zone.
—Tom Ingles, Puyallup High School

So what!
—Paul Wallrof, University of Puget Sound

Do not be afraid. Do not be discouraged.
—Mike London, College of William and Mary

Faith, family, and football.
—Mike London, College of William and Mary

Play for the audience of one.
—Brian Jensen, Bellarmine Preparatory School

It can be done.
—Kris Diaz, Baldwin Wallace University

Make full my joy, that ye be of the same mind, having the same love, being of one accord, of one mind. (Philippians 2:2)
—Randy Davis, Orting High School

American ends in "I can."
—Phil Hayford, Keswick Christian School

The Ten Commandments didn't come à la carte.
—Phil Hayford, Keswick Christian School

Next play.
—Kurt Keener, Gilbert Christian School

God's gift to you is your physical attributes; your gift to God is what you do with them.
—Kurt Keener, Gilbert Christian School

We play for a sovereign God who already knows the outcome, so play free without fear of making a mistake.
—Bobby Miller, Life Christian Academy

We cannot control what happened on the last play, good or bad. The most important play of the game, and the only one that counts, is the next one.
—Sam McCorkle, Oxford High School

The sky is the limit.
—Eddie Jones, Blinn College

The losing coach must watch his dreams of victory slide by and think of the next game and a new chance to win. He must never give up hope of victory, because how can a team believe in winning if the coach doesn't believe it?
—Richard L. Hardy

The next play is the most important play.
—K. C. Johnson, Adna High School

Worry only about the things that we can control. Do not waste time and energy worrying about things outside our control.
—Rick Jones, Greenwood High School

Bulldogs never bow down.
—Rick Jones, Greenwood High School

Whether you think you can or think you can't, you are right.
—Henry Ford, Ford Motor Company

Sometimes, not nearly enough, we get a chance to be part of something greater than ourselves, and it starts with a belief that we can.
—Ron Stolski, Brainerd High School

Give the ball a chance.
—Bill Ralston, youth baseball
    [Good things can happen when you hit a fair ball.]

Concentrate and focus. You can do it.
—Bill Ralston, youth baseball

Faith, family, friends, and football.
—Tommy Mueller, Texas Christian University

If you think you can or can't, you're right.
—Dave Nelson, Minnetonka High School

Every battle is won before it's ever fought.
—Sun Tzu, Chinese military

Hope is the anchor of our soul.
—Skip Hall, Boise State University

The hay is in the barn. We are ready.
—Sid Otton, Tumwater High School

Play the next play, not the last play.
—Sam Knopik, Pembroke High School

QUESTIONS TO AFFECT YOUR LIFE

1) What role does faith play in your life? In whom and what do you have faith?

2) When did you realize the significance of faith? What or who was influential in leading you to this realization?

3) When you speak of faith, what is a favorite example or story from your own life that you can share with others?

4) Have you ever placed your faith in someone or something and been disappointed? How has this affected the way you approach faith today?

5) What advice would you give others about the importance or influence of faith?

TRAINING

- The action of teaching a person or animal a particular skill or type of behavior
- Training is teaching or developing in oneself or others any skills and knowledge that relate to specific useful competencies. Training has specific goals of improving one's capability, productivity, and performance.[4]
- To teach someone to do a particular job or activity[5]
- Organized activity aimed at imparting information and/or instructions to improve the recipient's performance or to help him or her attain a required level of knowledge or skill[6]
- The act, process, or method of one that trains; the skill, knowledge, or experience acquired by one that trains[7]
- To develop or form the habits, thoughts, or behavior of (a child or other person) by discipline and instruction; to make proficient by instruction and practice, as in some art, profession, or work; to give the discipline and instruction, drill, practice, etc., designed to impart proficiency or efficiency; to undergo discipline and instruction, drill, etc.[8]
- The education, instruction, or discipline of a person or thing that is being trained[9]
- Synonyms: instruction, teaching, coaching, tutoring, schooling, drilling, priming, preparation, guidance, indoctrination; exercise, exercises, physical workout, working out, bodybuilding, preparation

Almost all training includes at least two people: the person being trained, and the person doing the training. The goal of the trainer is not only to teach skills but also to elevate the performance of the trainee.

We have access to unlimited real-life and dramatized experiences via television, the internet, and social media, giving us the opportunity to observe the performance outcomes of countless athletes, musicians, actors, and speakers. What we often don't see, however, are the hours and sometimes years of training that led to the particular outcome on display, and we seldom know who the trainers were. For example, you might turn on your television or device and see an accomplished musician deliver a beautiful performance of a powerful classic, and your reaction might be, "Wow, what talent!" But you are seldom provided with any background on what type of training the musician received, how much, and from whom.

It is a recognized fact that few people achieve significant success alone. Interview any accomplished athlete, musician, or artist, and I guarantee his or her story includes at least a handful of coaches, teachers, or trainers who helped develop their ability or facilitated opportunities for their success. Most success depends, at least in part, on the expertise of trainers who helped to refine the performance to its highest potential. Fulton Buntain, the senior pastor at Life Center in Tacoma, used to say, "If you see a turtle on a fence post, he didn't get there by himself."

PARENTS: PARTNERS IN TRAINING

Among the most significant influencers and trainers of future stars are their parents. In fact, according to the Bible, training is part of a parent's job description. Proverbs 22:6 says, "Train up a child in the way he should go, and when he is old he will not depart from it" (NKJV).

Both of my sons took piano lessons in elementary school. Ronni and I selected the teacher, paid for the lessons, and took the boys to and from the home of the teacher, but learning to play the piano really depends on the student and the teacher. My sons learned the basics from their teacher; whatever understanding and ability they gained from those lessons was the result of that teacher's expert insight into how to teach them to effectively play the piano. From there, it was up to them. If they wanted to improve their skills, they needed to apply what they learned from their teacher by practicing at home. Good opportunity, good instruction, good learning, and good application were all key elements of developing the boys' skills.

Why do outstanding young musicians often develop in the homes of adult musicians? Because the parents provide the early training and awareness needed for their children to be successful. Good friends of mine, Kenton and Benita Lee, have spent their careers in the music field. All four of their children attended and graduated from Life Christian Academy. Not surprisingly, all four became excellent musicians and were a blessing to our school's performing arts program. Today, years after their graduation, they continue to perform in a variety of contexts.

Where did it all start? In the home of Kenton and Benita with their diligent training. I witnessed many concerts in which the Lee children put on an excellent performance with their peers. Like the rest of the audience, I did not see the hundreds of hours of instruction and the disciplined practice that had been necessary for those children to achieve success with their voices or instruments. Kenton and Benita provided the training to their children, and the rest of us enjoyed the outcome!

Similarly, renowned golfer Tiger Woods's success was significantly influenced by his father. Earl Woods spent thousands of hours guiding Tiger's development as a young golfer, including purchasing the necessary equipment and contributing his time to help Tiger develop an appreciation and love for the game. Recently I heard the story of some of Tony Finau's earliest golf training experiences. His father had provided golf clubs, put a mattress against an inside wall of their garage, and then gave Tony and his brother full access to their indoor "driving range."

Today, when we watch Tiger Woods or Tony Finau play on the

PGA tour, we marvel at their ability, talent, and achievement. What isn't on display, and what we may never discover, is the extent of their fathers' involvement in their training, as well as others who subsequently trained them.

COACHES AND STUDENTS: TRAINERS AND TRAINEES

Coaches play a significant role in training people who aspire to higher levels of achievement. Name virtually any pursuit or activity, and there is almost certainly a coach or trainer you can hire to help you improve your efforts.

At its most basic level, coaching involves the effective teaching of fundamental concepts, as well as the drills and repetition needed to develop the fundamental skills. A coach also provides a level of expectation and accountability that isn't present when someone is learning or pursuing something independently. Influential coaches deliver encouragement along with their training that helps their trainees stay the course and push through barriers, propelling them onward to higher achievement. The best coaches not only have a high level of expertise and skill but are also passionate about bringing out the best in others.

What characterizes the best student or trainee? Diligence, dedication, and determination. Over more than four decades of coaching and leading, I have encountered numerous athletes, students, teachers, and others who rose to high levels of achievement not because of their innate talent, but because of their diligence in training. Their willingness to train, even when others were absent, resulted in the drive and determination necessary to achieve at their highest level possible.

BE THE BEST AT GETTING BETTER

I first met Mark Nellermoe when he was a high school senior and football player at Fargo North, where he was coached by Dave Heide. Though he had played largely in the shadow of teammate Mark

Speral, who became an outstanding quarterback at North Dakota State University, Mark Nellermoe's high school achievements gained the attention of our NDSU coaching staff and merited a partial scholarship to join the Bison football program.

Once Mark joined the team, I worked with him to continue building and refining his skills. He was an adept runner in our veer option offense, but he needed to improve his ability to throw the football. Mark was an eager learner, brought significant focus to every practice, and was fun to coach. It was also enjoyable to watch his development as a passer.

Most importantly, let me describe another element of Mark's training that most people never saw. His commitment to improving included hundreds of hours in our weight room and individual workouts on the turf in summer conditioning. Mark was so disciplined that even on the hottest days in July, when most people were at the lakes, he was in the weight room. Many times I saw Mark leaving the turf field, his T-shirt drenched after conditioning and agility work preceded by two hours of weightlifting. Mark had an extreme passion to succeed, and he had the discipline to train his body for opportunity on the football field.

What was the result of Mark's diligent training? In 1981, three games into the season, our team had already lost two games, and the coaching staff decided to move Mark into the starting quarterback position. His level of training had shown his commitment to winning; every coach and player knew that he would give his best.

Game four of the season pitted our struggling Bison team against the number-one-ranked and undefeated University of North Dakota Sioux. It was a beautiful Saturday night at Dacotah Field. The stands were filled with Bison and Sioux fans, many of whom assumed that the Sioux would win the annual rivalry game. However, as the game clock advanced and the score remained close, the Bison team, led by its new starting quarterback, gained confidence. That confidence, along with inspired play by Mark and his teammates, resulted in fourth-quarter dominance that saw the Bison team take the lead and ultimately capture a 31–7 victory. I will never forget the hysteria on the field and in the locker room after that huge upset.

What had Mark Nellermoe contributed? Not glowing passing statistics, but steady, disciplined leadership of our offense, and inspiring efforts that his teammates knew reflected his commitment to training to be his very best. That NDSU team went from a 1–2 season start to winning ten games in a row led by Mark Nellermoe, and in December they played for the national championship in McAllen, Texas. Mark went on to lead the Bison to twenty-two wins out of twenty-four starts as the team's quarterback. It was a memorable journey for the team and a powerful result of Mark's self-disciplined training to prepare himself.

HARD WORK WORKS

Life Christian Academy had the privilege of hiring Matt Foreman to teach high school English shortly after he graduated from college. Matt also agreed to lead our strength and conditioning workouts for student-athletes. Having taught himself weightlifting in high school (including checking out a book from the city library), he had become a nationally competitive lifter who barely missed qualifying for the US Olympic Team. We were fortunate to have someone of Matt's expertise at our relatively new school.

One of the first students to inquire about weightlifting, during his eighth-grade year, was Jeff Theorell. Like many students in the middle years of their education, Jeff was struggling with his identity as a young person. At that time, our school had no designated building space for a weight room. Instead, a semitrailer parked on the property housed our bench press, weights, and dumbbells. Talk about humble beginnings! This is where Jeff first approached Matt with his interest in weightlifting.

Matt could tell from the first conversation that Jeff had the passion to pursue weightlifting, which Matt described as "not a glory, fans-in-the-stands type of sport." Jeff got permission to be dismissed from school five minutes early to unlock the trailer and turn on the lights and heat in preparation for the other students' arrival. This initiative and determination showed Matt that weightlifting was important to Jeff.

Over the ensuing months, Matt's training techniques and Jeff's commitment to weightlifting led to strength gains for the eighth grader. It was obvious to many of us that Matt was helping Jeff develop into a strong, well-disciplined young man. In addition to playing football and weightlifting, Jeff also competed in track and field as a successful shot putter.

In time, Matt asked if the school could start a competitive powerlifting team. We did so, which created a whole new level of opportunity for athletes such as Jeff to compete against the best from other schools and clubs. Jeff became successful, winning several competitions, two state powerlifting championships, and a USA Powerlifting National Championship in his freshman year of college. He was inducted into Life Christian Academy's Alumni Association Hall of Fame in the fall of 2018 for his significant achievement.

What began with a conversation in a semitruck trailer between Jeff Theorell and Matt Foreman became a substantial training program that had a positive effect on many students. When I asked Jeff to describe the role Matt played in his development, his response was, "Matt Foreman believed in me before I believed in myself. His confidence that I could do it reinforced my effort to improve and continue pressing toward my goals." Jeff's diligence and commitment to powerlifting, combined with the training he received from Matt, resulted in his reaching the pinnacle of achievement as a state and national champion.

The teacher and the student: both need to be invested if either is to be successful! To this day, Matt and Jeff remain in contact, and it does not surprise me that they are each advancing similar objectives three decades later.

Today Matt continues to deliver high-level training through his Core CrossFit program in Phoenix, Arizona. Based on the knowledge he has acquired over thirty-five years, Matt's approach is firm and he requires his clients to follow his plan for their development and success. He is the expert, and people pay for his expertise, not his opinion. In addition to their awareness of his high expectations, Matt's people know he cares for them and wants the very best for them. His philosophy and desire are to help his clients not only navigate the path to success and fulfillment of their fitness goals, but also apply good habits and discipline to other aspects of their lives. Recently Matt was inducted into the Arizona Weightlifting Hall of Fame for his achievement and his influence on the people he has trained over many years.

Jeff Theorell is now the owner of Jeffit Transformation, a successful fitness coaching enterprise through which he invests in people seeking coaching and direction. As part of a partnership called The 300 Club Elite (the300club.net), Jeff also developed and implements a system of accountability and growth called FREE, an acronym for Fitness, Relationships, Education, and Economics—four areas of life with which many people struggle. A key aspect of the program is helping clients determine their "why" in each of these areas and then develop specific goals.

PRACTICE WITH PURPOSE

Another Life Christian Academy graduate who has exemplified achievement through rigorous training, first as a student and now as an alumnus, is Amy Frederick Palmquist. Amy began participating in athletics as a middle school student. As a high schooler, she worked hard to develop her abilities as an athlete. She became an excellent volleyball player and also competed in basketball and softball. By her senior year, Amy had become an accomplished multisport athlete and received several commendations, including being named the Pierce County Female High School Athlete of the Year in 2002. She was the first in the region from a relatively small school to win this prestigious award sponsored by the Tacoma Athletic Commission.

One of Amy's first coaches was Chuck Carone, a physical education teacher and longtime volleyball coach at LCA. Chuck's recollection of Amy as a middle-school and high-school athlete includes adjectives such as *humble*, *focused*, *determined*, and *team-oriented*. Amy was a pleasure to coach because of her determination to train, practice, and lead by example. She was a real asset to the teams on which she played.

Following her graduation from LCA, Amy attended St. Martin's University, where she continued her physical training regimen while also competing in athletics. She sought opportunities to pursue her passion—physical training and fitness—with increased focus. Realizing she wanted to build a career as the owner of an exercise and fitness facility, Amy left St. Martin's University to pursue a degree in exercise science and nutrition at Eastern Washington University.

Upon attaining her bachelor's degree, Amy accepted a position as a fitness instructor and coach at a fifty-five-and-over community fitness facility, where she began crafting her training of others. She also continued to train personally with great discipline and focus on nutrition. Four years later, Amy was ready to open her own facility. Located in Lacey, Washington, Transformation Fitness (transformationpt.com) now serves approximately three hundred clients each week. Amy is also sponsored by Nutrishop USA, whose wellness products she represents.

When I spoke with Amy recently, she said that her high school peers had believed in her and that she, in turn, had believed what they said to her. Over time, she became a self-motivated person who recognized that training and nutrition were key to her future success. I have heard many friends and fellow alumni speak with high regard for Amy's achievement of an exceptional level of fitness, a direct result of her disciplined training for years, dating back to her high school experience.

Leveraging her personal passion, Amy has created a culture at Transformation Fitness that challenges athletes and other people to think differently about themselves and take action to become who they want to be. Part of this is helping clients to recognize what they are not doing on their own and to remove any obstacles holding them back. Amy teaches her team to help clients come to believe that they can establish new behaviors and then take action to make it happen. As early as their first appointment, clients implement one or two fundamental changes that quickly begin delivering results. Amy's team then works alongside to help build on that first step, and the next. The mission of Transformation Fitness is "transforming lives from the inside out"—an honorable endeavor on many levels!

Chuck Carone went on to become a corporate fitness coach for employees at Intuit, a large San Diego–based corporation with its own fitness facility on the campus. Chuck was hired to develop and implement physical training and wellness programs that would help employees sustain their efforts and teams in the workplace. When I spoke with Chuck about training, he preferred to refer to his role as coaching. His job, as he perceived it, was to coach Intuit employees in fitness and wellness. To achieve success, Chuck said, employees needed to cultivate (1) belief in the system, (2) belief in themselves, and (3) belief in their coach. In his experience, the employees, representing a variety of ages, really wanted to be coached. They would then transfer the coaching they received to the teams they were part of Monday through Friday in the corporate challenge.

I believe Chuck's passion for fitness and wellness, beginning with his teaching at Life Christian Academy, led to his subsequent work in the corporate employee fitness arena. In both environments, the same principles of training with discipline and instruction accomplished the desired outcome of helping people improve performance and achieve greater success on multiple levels.

ONLY YOU CAN CONTROL YOUR EFFORT

Corporate America spends millions of dollars on training programs for new employees. Rachel Golden, former student body president at Life Christian Academy, now works for Intel Corporation. Rachel recently received a promotion at the company's facility in Chandler, Arizona, which employs approximately four thousand employees. In my visit with Rachel, I learned her team had encouraged her to get out of her comfort zone and seek greater opportunity within the

Intel campus. Deciding to take their advice, she earned not only a promotion but also a raise.

One of Rachel's next steps, in accepting the responsibilities of her new position, is to engage in a significant amount of training. Similar to several examples cited in this chapter, Rachel's training will not merely provide her with skills necessary for her new assignment, but will also help her apply her abilities in ways that serve a greater number of people and deliver more value for Intel. Rachel also feels the training will benefit her career overall.

DO WHAT YOU CAN, WHERE YOU ARE, WITH WHAT YOU HAVE

As the head football coach at the University of Puget Sound, I was aware of many outstanding high school football players in our recruiting area. One was Jason Chorak, a four-year starter at Vashon High School, on a small island in the South Puget Sound. One of my assistants, Paul Wallrof, lived on Vashon Island and frequently updated our coaches on the latest achievements of "this Chorak kid," a dominant player in the Nisqually League. Many schools from around the country recruited Jason, who ultimately elected to play for Don James at the University of Washington.

When I interviewed Jason about his small-school training workouts in high school, he said he spent a lot of time playing racquetball, which he credits with building his quick burst, reaction time, and lateral movement ability. Jason's daily summer training routine comprised working for his dad's construction company, followed by playing a few hours of racquetball and then lifting weights at his high school to further develop his strength.

At UW, Jason was heavily influenced by Bill Gillespie, a successful weightlifter and great role model. Jason said, "Bill knew I was country strong, and he could see I wanted to work hard to get to the next level." Jason credits the Husky program with preparing him for the National Football League, from coaching to training and conditioning. Jason became an All-American for the Husky defense and then played for Dick Vermeil with the St. Louis Rams and Jim

Mora with the Indianapolis Colts. His journey from little Vashon High School to the NFL is legendary in terms of the amount of training and development in which he engaged to become his very best. Thanks, Jason, for being an example to others!

As I mentioned at the outset of this chapter, each of these examples of training and the outcomes they produced includes two elements: people willing to be trained in order to perform at higher levels, and effective trainers willing to invest their knowledge and experience in another person. When it comes to achieving excellence and success, it's been my experience that the will to succeed depends in great part on training. Would you agree?

I challenge you to think of that influential coach, teacher, or mentor who has helped you become who you are today. The expressions or sayings in this book all come from people of influence. Their words become part of the training and development of their students.

SAYINGS

Hard work is not a form of punishment.
—Dick Vermeil, St. Louis Rams

How a team plays is determined by its individual players' commitment to improvement in practice.
—Rick Noren, St. Martin's University

Compete always and in all ways.
—Mile Hookstead, University of Dubuque

As an offensive line coach, I like to remind our players to "walk with their feet straight." They'll become better players, and it will help them when they ask girls for dates.
—George Papageorgiou, Benedictine College

Luck is nothing more than the residue of hard work.
—Vince Lombardi, Green Bay Packers

Assignment, technique, and effort on each play.
—Tom Merrill, John F. Kennedy High School

If you are not straining, you are not gaining.
—Mickey Andrews, Florida State University

Practice with a purpose.
—Carey Bogue, Life Christian Academy

This ain't no holiday.
—Mike Durnin, University of Dubuque

We will work while our opponents sleep.
—Steve Buuck, Faith Lutheran Middle School and High School

The repetitions we practice are done in such a way that you're automatic on game day.
—Steve Cain, University of Puget Sound

Do the work.
—Chris McCrory, Amory High School

Luck is what happens when preparation meets opportunity.
—Seneca, a Roman philosopher, and Robert Hunt, University of Puget Sound

Good enough is not good enough. You have to do a little bit extra to be better than anyone else.
—Tom Sanchez, South Bend High School

Let the other guy get tired.
—P. J. Fleck, University of Minnesota

Be the best at getting better.
—Eric Taylor, Cincinnati Hills Christian Academy

The essence of blocking is the contact point and the finish point.
—Pat Simmers, North Dakota State University

What you see is what you taught. It doesn't matter what we told a player. If he is doing something wrong, we didn't teach him properly.
—Leo Ringey, North Dakota State University

We love it.
—Dave Collins, Hope Community Church

Keep your elbow up—generally sound advice for most athletic skills.
—Sam Knopik, Pembroke High School

Double duty guys. Appreciate the grind.
—Greg Polnasek, Albion College

No one ever drowned in sweat.
—Courtney Meyer, Concordia University, Nebraska

You're only as good as we practice.
—Mike Breeden, Heritage Christian Academy

Get your fat dirty.
—Mike Anderson, University of Wisconsin Lacrosse
   [on pad level on run blocking]

Apple bobber.
—Mike Anderson, University of Wisconsin Lacrosse
   [on head movement on pass protection]

Only you can control your effort.
—Bill Diedrick, high school and college coach

Hit and hustle.
—Rick Giampietri, Central Valley High School

Faster, harder, and smarter than yesterday.
—Travis Niekamp, Illinois State University

Create your own atmosphere.
—Stephanie Dunn, Mt. Paran Christian School

Hard work works.
—Brian Jensen, Bellarmine Preparatory School

I may play against someone who is better than I am, but I'll never run against one who is going to be in better condition.
—John Wooden, University of California, Los Angeles

You will play on game day the way you practice during the week.
—George Allen, Washington Redskins

QUESTIONS TO AFFECT YOUR LIFE

1) Who do you know to be an excellent trainer of people?

2) If you were looking for an effective trainer, what characteristics would be most important in that person?

3) How do you think Jeff Theorell transformed from an introverted, struggling, middle-school student to a state champion in high school?

4) To which of the sayings in this chapter do you most relate?

DISCIPLINE

- The practice of training people to obey rules or a code of behavior, using punishment to correct disobedience
- To train someone to obey rules or a code of behavior using punishment to correct disobedience
- To train oneself to do something in a controlled and habitual way
- Synonyms: control, regulation, direction, order, authority, rule, strictness, routine, regimen, teaching instruction, drill, drilling, exercise; train, drill, teach, school, coach, educate, regiment, indoctrinate

Growing up on a farm, I learned at an early age the essence of discipline. One of my jobs as a boy was to keep our cows in the pastures. Two levels of discipline were necessary to fulfill this responsibility: one for me, and one for the cows.

First, I needed to ensure that the fences on the border of the pasture acreage were well constructed, well maintained, and constantly monitored for loose or broken wires. My father taught me that a tight fence was a major deterrent to any animal trying to break out of the pasture. Part of my job as a young boy was to walk miles of fence to inspect for any broken wires or loose posts that might tempt a cow or calf. It was my responsibility to be disciplined in evaluating the fence carefully and consistently.

Second, once a cow discovered how to break through a bad spot in the fence, the same animal was likely to wander along the fence lines looking for other weak spots where it would attempt another break. My father taught me that it all started with a solid fence kept secure to remove temptation for the animals.

Is this example not a microcosm of life? When we are in a disciplined routine with clear expectations, our nature is to focus on the benefits of a structured life and the "grass" in front of us. As parents, leaders, or coaches, we need to establish structure, expectations, and disciplines for those we lead in order to help them reach goals and overcome challenges. This includes everything from parenting consistency between two parents to policy handbooks, communication, and daily expectations such as work hours, break times, and monitoring of production within a group of people. The old saying "What gets measured gets done" is really about the discipline of evaluating performance. This begins with the leader establishing and following up on clear expectations.

SMALL DETAILS DECIDE BIG GAMES

The development of daily disciplines or habits is the means by which desired outcomes become part of our performance. When I was a young boy, my parents had expectations—called *chores*—for me. My responsibility to the family was to complete my chores in a timely and effective manner.

Parenting includes the establishment and enforcement of discipline within the family structure, wherein all members of the family have responsibilities. When those responsibilities are fulfilled well, the family unit is cohesive, interdependent, and subservient to one another. Conversely, when children are given no responsibility, they wander through life with little or no respect for authority and lacking accountability for completing simple tasks. I have always believed that little things done well lead to greater opportunities. The person who does not take care of small responsibilities is unlikely to graduate to the big things in life.

With athletic teams, coaches must establish expectations that become part of the team's culture. How many times have we heard the expression "They won because they were the more disciplined team"? Discipline does not show up just on game day, but instead is exhibited in daily routines, practices, and each individual's responsibilities to the team.

In football, for example, a simple scheme is training for the first play of the game. Every game begins with one team kicking the ball from their own 35-yard line and the other team receiving it. A successful kickoff includes three dynamics:

1. An effective kicker. A player who can kick the ball deep, with hang time, and to a consistent location on the field puts the return team at a disadvantage.

2. Discipline within the kickoff coverage team. Most coaches teach these ten players that they each must "maintain their lane" while running down the field to cover the kick. In theory, each of the ten has a responsibility to discipline himself to sprint down the field while maintaining a five-yard distance between himself and the teammates on either side of him. Losing this five-yard distance results in a gap or soft spot in the coverage, creating a space for the return team to exploit as they attempt to run to open field. Coaches drill this discipline into the kickoff team during team meeting rooms and on the practice field.

3. Making the tackle. It does no good for ten players to run down the field if they miss the ball carrier. The discipline to run fifty yards while maintaining sufficient control to make the tackle results in successful team coverage of the kick.

Three disciplines are required: a proper kick by the kicker, proper lane discipline by the coverage personnel, and tackling the ball carrier. The best kickoff coverage teams master all three and execute them consistently.

IT'S ALL ABOUT THE PROCESS

Most businesses and nonprofit organizations build strategic plans for the implementation of initiatives that will stimulate growth, better production numbers, and increased overall effectiveness. Strategic plans can cost thousands of dollars for consultants, as well as many hours of employee and stakeholder time—which can be even more valuable than money.

My experiences helping organizations create strategic plans also call for best practices in implementing the plans. These practices include a timeline for initiating and completing key steps in the plan and an oversight committee to monitor the effectiveness of the plan and document progress on its implementation. Most strategic plans have a lifespan of three to five years. The oversight committee performs its function with regular meetings that focus on the plan and periodic reports to owners, board members, and key stakeholders. In essence, the oversight committee keeps the plan "alive and present" to its people.

Unfortunately, many organizations fail to adopt the necessary discipline to effectively implement and monitor the success of their strategic initiatives. It's not uncommon to hear an employee or board member say, "Yes, we did a strategic plan, but I don't know what happened to it," or, "Oh, I think it's on John's shelf somewhere." This is a sad indicator of good intentions but lack of discipline in follow-through. Spending the money and time to create a strategic plan is admirable, but subsequent failure to implement it is counterproductive and demoralizing. One best practice to prevent a lack of follow-through is to publish a "presentation copy" of the plan to stakeholders, which increases awareness and accountability. Being transparent creates the expectation of follow-through. It's called organizational discipline—internal and external.

When many people hear the word *discipline*, they think of rules, but rules are not an end unto themselves. Instead, rules—often in the guise of policies and guidelines—are a means by which teams and organizations establish a culture for meeting goals and achieving success. In my opinion, rules should be positively created and monitored, and key updates on progress and achievements communicated on a timely basis. The better that leaders communicate progress—or wins—to their people, the better their teams will respond. Well-executed rules, policies, and guidelines are perceived as strengths of a unit, team, or organization.

Studies of today's success formulas for businesses and teams include an increased emphasis on "trusting the process." In reality, trusting the process involves developing disciplines, procedures, and evaluation tools that support progress toward a goal. The day-to-day journey is the process, and the goal may be a big win on game day, an outstanding quarterly report, or an annual report that shows goals met or exceeded for the year. Each of these results shows that the process worked effectively for the team or organization. Hereto, this is a reinforcement of the disciplines needed within a unit, team, or organization.

The process is built on good disciplines executed well. The best people yearn for discipline; they know that to be successful, they must work the process, which includes rules, policies, and guidelines for achievement.

WHO YOU ARE WHEN NO ONE IS LOOKING

People develop self-discipline within their own process and drive to succeed. In my search for self-discipline teaching, I ran across a blog post titled "Self-Discipline Is the Foundation for Success." The author, Syed Balkhi, is a Pakistani American named as one of the top-100 entrepreneurs under the age of thirty in the entire world. Here's what Syed writes about self-discipline:

> I've met and talked with some of the most amazing entrepreneurs. All these successful people shared a common character trait: self-discipline ...
>
> Self-discipline is the ability to control your impulses and be able to make yourself do things that need to be done ... In my opinion, self-discipline is the foundation for success ... The more

self-disciplined you are, the easier it is to reach your hardest goals.[10]

Well said, Syed!

The best teams or organizations are those with self-disciplined people, so hiring, coaching, and leading self-disciplined people are key steps to success. As a football coach of thirty-five years, I remember well how rewarding and effective it was to help my players develop self-discipline for their training, roles, and execution of their assignments, as well as collective self-discipline as a team. Self-disciplined teams with high goals are hard to defeat. Why? Because they have put so much into the effort that they will not be beaten, and they do not beat themselves.

The poem below speaks to the reality of a life guided by disciplined focus on the day-to-day choices we each encounter. Our lives become a picture of these choices, good or bad. Cultivating the discipline to consistently make the best choices for all whom your life affects can serve as a lightning rod for a life lived well.

> You may bring to your office and put in a frame
> A motto as fine as its paint,
> But if you're a crook when you're playing the game,
> That motto won't make you a saint.
> You can stick up the placards all over the wall,
> But here is the word I announce;
> It is not the motto that hangs on the wall,
> But the motto you live that counts.
>
> If the motto says smile and you carry a frown,
> Do it now and you linger and wait;
> If the motto says help and you trample men down;
> If the motto says love and you hate;
> You won't get away with the mottoes you stall.
> For truth will come forth with a bounce—
> It is not the motto that hangs on the wall,
> But the motto you live that counts.[11]

Discipline, for many people, is a negative word. Yet I can cite story after story that clearly illustrate that discipline is one of the significant keys to personal and organizational success. Rules and discipline can bring positive results within your life, family, team, or business! Would you agree?

SAYINGS

> *Watching a player every day in practice gives you much better insight into his capabilities than watching him in a game. You know his physical limitations, and more important, you study him as a person and get to know his mental limitations. As a result, we rarely are surprised by what a player shows us in a game. We know him best from practice.*
> —Bud Grant, Minnesota Vikings

> *And in truth, I've never known a man worth his salt who in the long run, deep down in his heart, didn't appreciate the grind, the discipline. There is something in good men that yearns for and needs discipline and the harsh reality of head-to-head combat.*
> —Vince Lombardi, Green Bay Packers

> *We may very well be the last bastion of discipline in the United States. The military doesn't have it the way it used to; schools, churches, and families don't have it. Athletics might be the only thing left where a young man, for two hours a day, yields himself to us because he wants to be part of a team. We tell him to discipline himself so that he loses himself for something bigger: the team. In that way, he actually becomes a better person.*
> —Ara Parseghian, University of Notre Dame

> *If you are always early, you are never late.*
> —Mike Van Diest, Carroll College

Our uniforms are all alike, even at practice. That's part of my discipline.
—John Wooden, University of California, Los Angeles

We need discipline. A coach can't be one of the boys.
—Tony Mason, University of Arizona

Do what you are supposed to do, when you are supposed to do it, and do it that way every time.
—Mike Van Diest, Carroll College

To get where you want to go, you've got to drive and push yourself relentlessly. You've got to want to win so badly that the thought of coming in second is simply intolerable. And you've got to pay the price for winning. Paying the price, in anything you do, is spelled "work." Days and nights and years of work. And it's too bad that many men—men born with basic talent—think of work as a dirty word.
—Bill Russell, Los Angeles Lakers

Always do more than is expected.
—Jerry Moore, Appalachian State

If you are not five minutes early, you're five minutes late.
—Mike Durnin, University of Dubuque

Okay, now do it again. And over and over again.
—Bill Manlove, Widener University

Be the best you can be in all that you do.
—Kris Diaz, Baldwin Wallace University

Life is short. Run to the ball.
—Jerry Rosburg, Baltimore Ravens

Do as I say, not as I do.
—Fred Manuel, Lane College

The athletic field is a big laboratory for experimentation in which the young man learns to discipline himself and experiments with himself against other men, mentally, emotionally, and physically. He learns lessons that cannot be taught in the classroom.
—Knute Rockne, University of Notre Dame

A walk is never a hustle.
—Ron Rood, Zillah High School

Play hard from the snap of the ball to the whistle.
—Larry Donovan, BC Lions
   [eight-second concept]

Keep on keeping on.
—Johnny Majors, University of Tennessee

Have some character, son; don't be one.
—Bobby Hauck, University of Montana

Honey hush.
—Larry Prather, Reinhardt University
   [after a great or awful play]

Miller time is fifteen minutes early.
—Dave Miller, Lakes High School

You can never go wrong doing what is right.
—Dave Miller, Lakes High School

Get out of the gates.
—Todd Bridge, Elma High School
   [meaning like a racehorse]

See it, say it, hear it, repeat it.
—Todd Bridge, Elma High School

Be where your feet are.
—Steve Amrine, Kelso High School, and Tom Coughlin,
  New York Giants

*Don't practice till we get it right, but until we can't get
it wrong.*
—Mike Breeden, Heritage Christian Academy

There is no right way to do the wrong thing.
—Courtney Meyer, Concordia University, Nebraska

DWR (Do what's right.)
—Courtney Meyer, Concordia University, Nebraska

Respond, don't react.
—Jeff Monken, U.S. Army

*Character—true character—is what you are when no
one is looking.*
—Ken Rucker, University of Texas

The stronger you are, the more courage you have.
—Johnny Watson, Little Rock Christian Academy

You don't need to be sick to get better.
—George Crace, Pacific Lutheran University

Why am I waiting?
—Ross Hjelseth, Life Christian Academy

Mental toughness is essential to success.
—Vince Lombardi, Green Bay Packers

Effort is the price of admission.
—Randy Hart, Stanford University

The hay is never in the barn.
—Mike Van Diest, Carroll College

Don't think; just go.
—Jovan Haye, Vanderbilt University

You need to concentrate to the performance level you want, not the level you are comfortable with.
—Rick Noren, St. Martin's University

If you're not early, you're late.
—Bill Alexander, Quincy High School

Play and practice as hard as you can as long as you can.
—Miles Hookstead, University of Dubuque

You can learn more character on the 2-yard line than anywhere else in life.
—Paul Dietzel, Louisana State University

Small details decide big games.
—Phil Hayford, Keswick Christian School

Shut up, get down, and give me ten push-ups.
—Tom Merrill, Kennedy High School

Don't be who they think we are.
—Benjamin Benavides III, John F. Kennedy High School

Speed beats man. Angles beat speed.
—Judd Keim, Pacific Lutheran University

Anyone can start a block, but only the best finish.
—Steve Cain, University of Puget Sound

Perfection isn't the goal. Progress is the goal.
—Steve Cain, University of Puget Sound

Alignment, assignment, finish.
—Steve Cain, University of Puget Sound

Do your job.
—K. C. Johnson, Adna High School

D. I. E. (Discipline. Intensity. Execution.)
—K. C. Johnson, Adna High School

Do right.
—Scott Smith, Legacy Christian Academy

Talk is cheap. Someday is never. Do it now.
—Bill Heglar, Interlake High School

There are those who can, and those who can't.
There are those who will, and those who won't.
We want those who can and will.
—Gary Darnell, American Football Coaches Association

If it needs to be done, do it.
—Gary Darnell, American Football Coaches Association

Pick the pitch up off the pitcher's shoulder—give the
batter a specific area to watch for the ball.
—Bill Ralston, youth baseball

Do the things you know to be right, and refuse to do the
things you know to be wrong.
—Jim Wacker, Texas Christian University

The one thing everyone can do is play hard.
—R. C. Slocum, Texas A & M University

Nothing good ever happens after midnight.
—Dave Nelson, Minnetonka High School

Don't confuse routine with commitment.
—Dave Nelson, Minnetonka High School, and Bill Parcells,
  New York Giants

Two things we don't want to happen today: we don't want to be out-hit or out-hustled.
—Hank Biesiot, Dickinson State University
[final words before taking the field]

The eye in the sky does not lie.
—Buck Nystrom, Michigan State University

It's all about the process.
—Luke Balash, North Pole High School

Finish.
—Sam Knopik, Pembroke High School

You cannot soar with the eagles if you hang with the turkeys.
—Bob Lucey, Curtis High School

Be the best at response-ability.
—Jeff Thomas, University of Puget Sound

QUESTIONS TO AFFECT YOUR LIFE

1) To what or whom do you attribute any level of discipline in your life?

2) Who is the most self-disciplined person you know? What do you admire about this person?

3) In what area of your life would you like to be more disciplined?

4) Which illustration in this chapter can you most relate to your life?

MOTIVATION

- A reason or reasons for acting or behaving in a particular way
- Desire or willingness to do something; enthusiasm
- The act or an instance of motivating, or providing with a reason to act in a certain way[12]
- Synonyms: motivating force, incentive, stimulus, stimulation, inspiration, impulse, inducement, incitement, spur, goad, provocation, enthusiasm, drive, ambition, initiative, determination, enterprise, sense of purpose

Motivation is the key. To what? To everything. To joyful journeys and successful outcomes. It is literally the "why" that gets you out of bed in the morning and doing whatever you do throughout each day. Motivation is the process of stimulating people to action to accomplish goals. Its English-language root is *motive*, which is defined as "a reason for doing something."

Synonyms for *motive* include *passion*, *purpose*, *drive*, and *inspiration*. These are examples of *intrinsic* motivation, which comes from within an individual. Motivation can also be *extrinsic*, whereby a person is influenced by outside forces. Examples of extrinsic motivation could include the promise of a promotion if a performance target is reached, or a vacation or indulgence item when enough money has been saved up.

Whether their motivation is intrinsic, extrinsic, or both, high achievers have high motivation and readily feed their desire to achieve and attain outcomes that hold value and meaning for them.

PURPOSE AND PASSION

In work, athletics, and many other areas of life, we are evaluated in terms of our successes and failures, wins and losses. Therefore it is essential that we motivate ourselves and the people with whom we aspire to achieve, including family members, colleagues, our work team, players, and generations to come.

There is a definite correlation between (1) people's purpose and passion, and (2) the intensity of their intrinsic motivation. In my career as an educator, minister, and coach, I have observed that people who have discovered their purpose have a higher level of self-motivation than those who lack direction. Their passion to accomplish their purpose, whether short- or long-term, provides elevated drive and determination because they have directed their journey toward a specific destination.

From students finding their purpose or pursuing mastery of skills to adults and leaders of programs reaching for new milestones, I have witnessed many people moving toward uncommon levels of success because of their passion to reach their goals. Their purpose and passion provide most of the motivation needed to continue their pursuit of excellence in their skill or program development. They establish success patterns instead of merely achieving occasional success.

One of my best friends, Don Gustafson, made an appointment to see me when I was the head football coach at the University of Puget Sound. I had met Don a few months earlier through a mutual acquaintance. He owned a carpet business, but he loved athletics. During a meeting in my office, Don asked how he could get involved in coaching. I suggested he look at opportunities in youth sports or seek an assistant coaching role in a school program. Two years later, when I began my work to create Life Christian Academy, I called Don to ask if he wanted to help coach at LCA, and he immediately welcomed the opportunity.

Don was on our very first Eagle boys' basketball coaching staff and on our baseball staff, and he became our first head golf coach. Now, twenty-six years later, Don has coached every year and also volunteers in many other ways at our school. He has sold his business, but his purpose and passion now align with his work at LCA—all as a valued volunteer. Don didn't need a paycheck to develop his passion for working with young people. He did it because of his love for athletics and helping develop youth into outstanding adults. Along the way, he coached nine state championship golf teams! It all started with a conversation about how he might find his way into coaching. In May 2018, Don received Life Christian Academy's prestigious Power of Commitment award recognizing his twenty-five years of significant volunteer efforts. His purpose became his passion, and his motivation came from being in the right place and position to effectively use both.

WORDS AND ACTIONS

Possibly the most important role played by leaders and coaches is that of motivator. Their personalities, goals, and motivation techniques are of primary importance in shaping the attitudes of team members and influencing the degree of success they will achieve. Leaders must develop their own philosophy of motivation and examine the means by which they inspire and direct those whom they lead.

Leaders must consider the following factors or processes in developing their philosophy of motivation:

1. what is most important to the success of the team, family, group, or organization;
2. motivation strategies and methods of implementing them;
3. how to make adjustments if the team does not respond positively to certain motivation techniques;
4. advantages and disadvantages of their motivation philosophy, since not everything works for everybody;
5. the effect of their words, style, and frequency of motivating, bearing in mind that strategies to motivate affect not only the organization, but also the individuals within it; and

6. willingness to personally practice their own philosophy beginning with themselves ("self-talk" and "team-talk" should be consistent and aligned).

Motivation usually presents in two forms, verbal and behavioral, and successful leaders effectively understand and implement both. Verbal motivation, more recognizable than behavioral, is typically the means by which people view the success of a leader's motivation style or philosophy. The most common types of verbal motivation are pep talks, team talks, and talks with individual team members. Verbal motivation works with varying degrees of effectiveness. Some leaders can speak clearly and dramatically in virtually any setting, whether the boardroom, executive meeting room, locker room, or family dinner table.

In their study titled "The Coach as Behavioral Engineer," Liskevych and Thorsteinson began with positive reinforcement as the reward for desired behavior. This positive interaction is probably the coach's most effective motivational tool. A major rule of behavioral psychology asserts that behaviors followed by positively rewarding actions are more likely to recur in the future. If a specific behavior is not followed by some type of reward, the likelihood of this behavior occurring in the future decreases. For leaders, being intentional about noticing positive behaviors and acknowledging them with positive feedback will result in more positive achievements. What we acknowledge gets noticed and replicated.[13]

As a coach and administrator, I often referred to these inspiring conversations with team members as "come to Jesus" meetings. In addition to intentionally preparing the content of my message, I worked diligently on my style and passion of delivery, evaluating my audience members and their potential responses. I knew that both the words and the style of communication would shape the effect of my message.

Grant Teaff was a very successful football coach at three universities, including Baylor. Shortly after leaving Baylor, he was offered the opportunity to become the executive director of the

American Football Coaches Association, a position he held for twenty-one years. Grant consistently reminded coaches of their influence on young people and our world. This poem, written by Coach Teaff, explains well this motivating influence:

> I dreamed a dream,
> but I had my doubts.
> "You can do it," he said.
> "I'll teach you how."
> I tried and tried;
> he said I should.
> I gave it my best;
> he knew I would.
> Lessons taught
> on the field of strife
> have been invaluable
> as I've faced life.
> When challenges
> come my way,
> I always think,
> What would he say?
> His inspiring words
> I hear even now,
> "You can do it.
> I taught you how."
> Now others dream
> and have their doubts.
> I say, "You can do it.
> I'll teach you how."[14]

The influence continues!

Behavioral motivation refers to inspiring people through actions, approaches, and methods. The broad spectrum of theories on behavioral motivation can be boiled down to emphasis on repetition, drill, and variety. All coaches will agree that players learn technique through drills that integrate the desired technique into their overall scope of proficiency. Players must appreciate the need for repetition and practice; however, the coach must know when to change the routine. At some point in the learning process, players become disenchanted with repeating the same practice drills ad infinitum. The effective motivator varies the approach to avoid players becoming bored with the routine. Variety, change, and a new environment all keep players motivated.

Similarly, an effective coach, while valuing consistency when it comes to preparing his team, also knows that when the same pregame talk is repeated over and over, it loses its authenticity and resonates poorly with the team. Halftime talks or end-of-quarter performance reviews with team members should be varied, fresh, and focused on the specific situation at hand.

Most importantly, the leader's motivation techniques must meet the needs of the team members, consistently helping and challenging them to achieve at superior levels during critical stages of the season or production cycle of work. Statements such as "He fires me up," "She had us ready to play," or "He challenged us to be at our best" are examples of positive perceptions of a leader's ability to motivate effectively. The players must remain enthusiastic about the mission of the team and the organization. Effective leaders consistently monitor their team's energy and drive to succeed, as well as studying individual players and their needs.

The most successful form of motivation comes from team members themselves. The players who are excited to play are those who want to participate and feel as though they are important to the success of the team. People who enjoy one another, a challenge, and the spirit of achieving at high levels will bring enthusiasm, energy, and a "We can do this" attitude to each day. Their desire for the challenge will serve as a motivator in itself.

A MATTER OF TIME

The movie *Miracle on Ice* tells the story of Herb Brooks's leadership of the 1980 USA Olympic ice hockey team and their journey to a gold medal. The "miracle" game took place during the medal round at the Winter Olympics in Lake Placid, New York, played between the United States team and the defending four-time gold medalist team from the Soviet Union.

The underdog USA team, composed of college players, had been selected and trained by Coach Brooks and his staff months earlier. He provided behavioral motivation by working hard himself, as did his coaches, and he drilled his team continuously for months leading up to the Olympics. The longer the team was together, the more the players believed in Coach Brooks's leadership because of his example to the team. Along the way, he also provided verbal motivation at key times during practices, early-round games, and then with increasing fervor and passion during the medal round. Most people were pleasantly surprised that the young USA team made it to the medal round of the Olympics competition—an achievement that superseded the USA's representation in this sport in most recent Olympic tournaments.

On the eve of the match between the USA and Soviet Union teams, Herb Brooks prepared his pregame team talk for the next day. He carefully chose words that would best prepare and motivate his players for the daunting challenge of facing the accomplished and highly esteemed Soviet Union team. Coach Brooks's locker room delivery of his pregame talk was a gleaming example of verbal motivation, and it has been featured in numerous publications as well as on YouTube and in the aforementioned movie. He challenged his team and told them, "This is your time." And indeed, it was, for the USA team defeated the Soviet team by a score of 4–3. Two days later, they defeated Finland 4–2 to clinch the hockey gold! In the years since, this feat has been celebrated as the culmination of Coach Brooks and his team coming together to do what no team had ever done. He was a motivator!

NUTS!

Another noteworthy example of verbal and behavioral motivation is the decision by Brigadier General Anthony McAuliffe when his 101st Airborne Division was surrounded and under siege in Bastogne, France, in World War II. After days of holding off German troops but gradually losing both ground and cover, McAuliffe received a message from the German officers asking if he wanted to surrender the encircled town. With just two hours to make a decision, he met with his officers, and they agreed to send a single-word reply to the Germans: "NUTS!" My father was one of the soldiers who survived that battle, and he told me it had been exciting to know they weren't giving up. At the same time, the reality that they would likely die in battle had been sobering.

The "battered bastards of Bastogne" endured, and days later, Bastogne remained under control of the Allied Forces. The simple, one-word answer from General McAuliffe had inspired his men to continue fighting for their cause: freedom. The Battle of Bastogne was one of the fiercest on the European front and a pivotal stakehold for the Allies.

PRAISE AND CRITIQUE

I have seen thousands of athletes respond to the demands of coaches. Sometimes these demands come in the form of exhortation to do your best. In other cases, coaches use verbal reprimands to call their players to higher levels of accountability. The most effective leaders and coaches understand that each person in their organization or team needs positive and negative reinforcement. Knowing how, when, why, and to whom to provide this reinforcement is a critical skill.

Part of the value of leaders being close to their teams is that they cultivate a keen instinct for the need for positive or negative reinforcement. The old axiom "Praise in public and critique in private" applies in most situations and prevents leaders from misusing their team members' respect. Knowing how, when, and why a team or individual needs reinforcement is crucial to the long-term success of leaders. Overreaction to a difficult or challenging situation can cost leaders credibility. The frequency of reinforcement can also be a key issue in terms of team morale. For instance, too many negative comments, corrections, or actions from leaders can cause their teams to become bitter instead of better.

In teams and organizations, seldom does a single person lower production or output. Leaders' ability to discern what or who is initiating a challenge equips them to determine how to best address the concern with the team or individual.

For every negative reinforcement or comment to a group or individual, it is important that a leader or coach follow up with encouragement. Positive reinforcement can instill a quality of team belief, behavior, and confidence that will last over an extended period of time. Timely correction, rather than ongoing criticism, is received as temporary disappointment in achievement level, couched in overall confidence and care. Correction followed by encouragement is a positive approach to addressing a challenge.

As a head football coach, I did my best to project a vision for success, hold assistant coaches and players accountable, and exhort everyone to do their best to succeed. I spent hours working on the talk that I would deliver to the team before kickoff on game day. I wanted my team's preparation for the game to be solid in every detail, and I believed that my role was to have them prepared mentally on game day. Most of my players would agree that this was a highlight of my coaching effort. My pregame talks were filled with "vim and vigor," as well as conviction and enthusiasm that we would play well and succeed! Go, Ranchers, Bison, Loggers, and Eagles!

When it came to correction or redirection, I always had to ask myself whether we were dealing with an isolated incident or an ongoing pattern. If something negative happened with an employee or team member, we worked through the issues surrounding the incident, corrected everything that could or needed to be corrected, and moved forward.

However, if a person or group was involved in a series of

misbehaviors, such as repeated tardiness or lack of compliance or production, the concern was significant and the resulting correction was likely to be of greater consequence and longer duration. The negative pattern had to be neutralized, which in some cases meant we had difficult decisions to make about the future of a team member or employee. For example, a pattern of being late to work or meetings sent a signal that the person did not respect the responsibility to be on time or the value of team time. Hereto, the leader's responsibility was to clarify the expectation, monitor the situation, and ensure the compliance of the person or group falling short.

In many instances, my corrective conversations with employees or team members took place in closed-door private meetings where we could address the issues frankly. If both the team member and I learned a bit more about the issue and left the room on a corrective course, the meeting was considered successful. In some cases, however, it is not clearly apparent that team members are willing and/or able to make the corrections needed to regain the trust and confidence of their organizations and other team members. At such times, it is up to leaders to use their discernment and take action accordingly. These are tough calls, but they come with the job and the responsibility.

I am a strong advocate for public praise. As both headmaster and head football coach, I tried to be intentional about "catching people in the act" of doing things right. From my perspective, it was my job to publicly acknowledge positive actions and achievements. We wrapped up every Life Christian Academy football practice with a few minutes of "'attaways," during which players acknowledged great effort or plays by teammates. We did the same after every game, regardless of the final score.

As LCA's headmaster, I implemented quarterly meetings of all employees to gather our team, enjoy a snack or treat together, recognize exceptional effort, and celebrate our collective wins and achievements. I believe the positive, uplifting reinforcement conveyed at those meetings was one of the reasons most of our high-quality faculty and staff continued investing their talents at LCA for many years.

I've never met a person who said they received too much encouragement. Have you? Positive words have positive effects and motivate people!

SAYINGS

Motivation—what we're really talking about here is motivating people, the ingredient that separates winners from losers—in football, and in anything.
—Paul "Bear" Bryant, University of Alabama

We have a motto in our group that we are going to play football with PhUN—physical, united, and nasty. Physical in their play, united in their knowledge, and nasty in their temperament. We discuss and expand on these three parts of the motto in order to keep the players engaged in their own development.
—George Papageorgiou, Benedictine College

It isn't necessary to see a good tackle. You can hear it.
—Knute Rockne, Notre Dame University

Row the boat!
—P. J. Fleck, University of Minnesota

I should never be able to tell the score of the game by how you are playing on the field. It could be 50–0 or 0–50; you will always play at your highest level.
—Dick Zatkovich, Lincoln High School

What a day! What a day!
—Jeff Thomas, University of Puget Sound

You have a responsibility to compete at your highest level for yourself and your team. The score will take care of itself.
—Dick Zatkovich, Lincoln High School

On a good day, I would congratulate the players on an outstanding practice, but I'd tell them that I hoped that would become their worst day ever as we continued to get better.
—Sam McCorkle, Oxford High School

We get better or worse every day; we never stay the same.
—Ross Hjelseth, Life Christian Academy

There's no game more important than the one we are playing today. What's the good of thinking about next week's game if we lose today?
—Ara Parseghian, University of Notre Dame

Shoot your bullets.
—Eddie Jones, Blinn College

Coach him, even if he is bad but your best. Don't ridicule; you can't trade them in. Build confidence. Praise.
—Tony Mason, University of Arizona

Great effort is expected and respected.
—Steve Cain, University of Puget Sound

It's all about you letting the door hit you where the good Lord split you.
—Rahman Sparks, Redan High School

Stay even keeled—don't get too high or too low.
—K. C. Johnson, Adna High School

Be positive in everything. Positive is a team concept. A strong team concept can beat a team with better athletes.
—Lou Holtz, University of Arkansas

Earn your reputation; make me have to play you.
—Chris McCrory, Amory High School

It's a beautiful day in the "wood." (When we get a chance to play the game of football with our buddies, it's a beautiful day, regardless of weather.)
—Rick Jones, Greenwood High School

The mediocre teacher tells. The good teacher explains. The great teacher inspires.
—Gary Darnell, American Football Coaches Association

I asked my team two questions frequently. First, "How do you feel?" and the only acceptable answer was "Great!" Second, "What number are you?" and the only answer was "Number one!" I always wanted my team and players to have a positive outlook.
—Mike Roberts, Franklin Pierce High School

The only things you can control are your attitude and your effort. So much (talent, injuries, etc.) is out of our hands. Take control of the things you can control.
—Tom Sanchez, South Bend High School

It is difficult to be great.
—John Mackovic, University of Texas

The moral is to the physical as three is to one.
—Napoleon Bonaparte

Play fast and finish.
—Eric Taylor, Cincinnati Hills Christian Academy

There is no set way to motivate a team, and the way I do it may be opposite your way.
—Paul "Bear" Bryant, University of Alabama

Don't say "Whoa" in a horse race.
—Pat Simmers, North Dakota State University

You are getting better or worse; you are never staying the same.
—Vernon Fox, Faith Lutheran High School

Some things are not as good as they seem. Some are not as bad as they seem. Somewhere in between is where reality falls.
—Lou Holtz, University of Notre Dame, and Kirk Talley, Warner University

Have fun.
—Sid Otton, Tumwater High School
[Last words before leaving the locker room to play]

He always talked about the "bottom line" of doing your job and playing with "calm intensity."
—Attributed to Mike Dunbar, University of California, Berkeley, by Jeff Zenisek, White River High School

What are you willing to give up?
—Jerry Moore, Appalachian State

You don't always get what you want, but you always get what you deserve.
—Mickey Andrews, Florida State University

Run to the fight.
—Brian Flattum, Cascade Christian School

Two pains in life: the pain of hard work, and the pain of regret. One goes away, and the other lasts a lifetime.
—Bill Beattie, Tumwater High School

Run to the roar.
—Mike London, College of William and Mary

Football is not a matter of life and death, but it is a matter of life.
—Jerry Rosburg, Baltimore Ravens

Motivate; do not manipulate.
—Pat Ruel, Seattle Seahawks

All attitudes are contagious, so be positive.
—Bubba Schweigert, University of North Dakota

Everything builds on everything.
—Stephanie Dunn, Mt. Paran Christian School

Leave it on the field.
—Mark Venn, Lindbergh High School

Bring the hammer.
—Brian Burdick, Charles Wright Academy
[the team's defensive mantra]

Approval is a great motivator. I try to follow up any criticism with a pat on the back, realizing that I cannot antagonize and influence at the same time.
—John Wooden, University of California, Los Angeles

Score. Never look back or stop during a play.
—Larry Donovan, BC Lions

Bigness is in the heart, anyway.
—Paul "Bear" Bryant, University of Alabama

The big time is not a place; it's a state of your heart. It's not something you get; it's something you begin.
—Frosty Westering, Pacific Lutheran University

Do it better than it's ever been done before.
—Chris Fisk, Central Washington University

Leave nothing to chance. It all matters.
—John Steigelmeier, South Dakota State University

Play to the best of your ability and beyond if necessary.
—Rick Giampietri, Central Valley High School

Play to win, playing those who deserve to play.
—Rick Giampietri, Central Valley High School

The harder you work, the luckier you get.
—John Cooper, Ohio State University

Tempo up.
—David Calloway, Central Methodist University

Energy, effort, and passion.
—David Calloway, Central Methodist University

Go hard or go home.
—Johnny Tusa, Waco High School

Motivation is teaching. You must convince the players your way is right. You must inspire learning.
—Chuck Knox, Seattle Seahawks

Nothing hard was ever easy.
—Gus Martin, Life Christian Academy

Be the best you can be, every day.
—Oval Jaynes, Wake Forest University

Your success is not just about changing your habits; it's about changing the way you think.
—Ben Newman, Newman Coaching

Give everything you've got. That's all it ever takes.
—Tim Camp, Eastern Oregon University

What we're talking about here, really, is motivating people. It's the ingredient that separates winners from losers—in football, in anything.
—Paul "Bear" Bryant, University of Alabama

Mental attitude and team morale are 90 percent of football.
—George Allen, Washington Redskins

You coach up. You treat them like men.
—Tony Mason, University of Arizona

A football player is a wonderful creature. You can criticize him, but you can't discourage him. You can defeat his team, but you can't make him quit. He is a hardworking, untiring young man doing the very best for his school or college. And when you come out of a stadium, grousing and feeling upset that your team has lost, he can make you feel mighty ashamed with two sincerely spoken words: "We tried."
—Charles Loftus, Yale University

It is one of the sad facts of our world that the man who announces a minor goal and reaches it is held in greater esteem than the man who attempts the spectacular and fails.
—unknown

Just playing with a championship team makes the rest of your life better.
—Dave DeBusschere, New York Knicks

We are in control of our mindset, not our opponents. We are in charge of the mental part of any game/match and how we react to the challenge.
—Janna Hjelseth, Tri-County High School

Football players love football.
—Eric Cohu, Little Rock Christian Academy

Hard work beats talent when talent doesn't work hard.
—Chris McCrory, Amory High School

True champions never look back. They stay HUNGRY.
—North Dakota State University locker room

QUESTIONS TO AFFECT YOUR LIFE

1) Give an example of a time when someone gave you significant encouragement or motivation.

2) What is your most vivid memory of receiving positive reinforcement? How did you respond?

3) What is your most vivid memory of receiving harsh correction? How did you respond?

4) Do you catch your family members or colleagues in the act of doing right, or do you most often catch them doing wrong? Which would you prefer to be caught in?

PERSEVERANCE

- Persistence in doing something despite difficulty or delay in achieving success
- Continued effort to do or achieve something despite difficulties, failure, or opposition[15]
- Steady persistence in a course of action or purpose especially in spite of difficulties, obstacles, or discouragement[16]
- Synonyms: persistence, tenacity, determination, resolve, resolution, resoluteness, staying power, purposefulness, firmness of purpose; patience, endurance, application, diligence, sedulousness, dedication, commitment, doggedness, pertinacity, assiduity, assiduousness, steadfastness, tirelessness, indefatigability, stamina

In the game of life, most of us encounter frequent challenges—pursuing an education, raising a family, competing to be chosen for a team, and so on. We're bound to face challenges and obstacles, and our ability to overcome them determines our degree of success in life. So much could be written on the topic of perseverance. All of the synonyms listed above relate to the staying power of life—our innate ability to push through challenges, small and large, to attain our goals.

My personal journey included growing up with an alcoholic father and, to compound the matter, living near the small community where I attended school. The older I got, the worse my dad's drinking got, and eventually most people in town knew about it. This became increasingly embarrassing for me, first as a young boy and then as a teenager. My mother, sister, and I spent significant time and effort trying to hide it, but we gradually realized that most people, including our close friends and neighbors, knew of my father's inability to say no to a drink.

At a relatively young age, I must have decided to overcome this challenge and focus on being the best person I could be in dealing with the unfortunate circumstances. I was thankful for my mother's perseverance as well, for she would not quit on either our family or my father. I learned from my mother about persistence, resolve, and faithfulness to her family and husband.

As a teenage athlete, I was apprehensive at games, fearing that my father would show up drunk. He never did so, but I remember looking around at the crowd during pregame warm-ups to see if he was in attendance during one of his drinking binges.

This was a life lesson. Later my father stopped drinking, and our relationship finished well. Looking back on those years, including many treatment center counseling sessions as a family, I can see now that these sessions were a testimony to perseverance, and my life has been better for the experience. At the time, however, I sure didn't think so!

One of my favorite reads of the past two years is Angela Duckworth's bestseller, *Grit: The Power of Passion and Perseverance*. This book outlines how grit is highly predictive of achievement throughout life. Duckworth explains in *Costco Connection* magazine, "I define grit as a combination of both perseverance and passion for long-term goals ... Not just working hard, but also loving what you do. Working hard on something you love. I study it because it's not the same as talent, which also helps you achieve great things in life but has hogged a disproportionate share of the spotlight in American culture." She encourages us all to be examples of the kind of character, strength, grit, and other things we want to encourage in our children and others.[17]

THE BEST YOU CAN FOR AS LONG AS YOU CAN

I saw perseverance firsthand in the life of Tyler Saugen, a student at Life Christian Academy for ten years during my tenure as headmaster. Doug and Vickie Saugen enrolled Tyler in preschool as a healthy, enthusiastic young boy who loved school and his new friends. For the first four years, Tyler developed on pace with his classmates and friends. I had a particularly keen view of his class because my son Tyler was in the same class—the eventual graduating class of 2007. Both Tylers attended school every day, achieved in the classroom, gained friends, attended birthday parties, and enjoyed life as young boys do.

In second grade, Tyler Saugen began experiencing occasional seizures. At first they were infrequent and short in duration, not appearing to have a long-term effect on his brain or body. Over the next several years, however, the seizures increased in frequency, extended in duration, and sometimes occurred at school in the presence of his classmates. With each seizure, his recovery took longer and the aftereffects grew more significant. Tyler's nerves and body began to show the effect of the stronger seizures as his motor skills, balance, and stability became significantly affected. At age eleven or twelve, Tyler began wearing a helmet for protection in case he fell, and his participation in sports, physical education, and certain school activities had to be curtailed.

Tyler's parents took him to the finest doctors in the Pacific Northwest to learn as much as they could about their son's seizures and what could be done to reduce their effects. I met with them numerous times for updates on the medical findings and to discuss any adjustments that needed to be made to the measures already in place. We all wanted Tyler to remain in our school as long as possible, and we wanted the best possible experience for him and his classmates.

In time, Tyler's parents decided to provide a caregiver to shadow him throughout his school experience. He also began receiving more individualized instruction and assistance through Life Christian Academy's LIFE (Learning Is For Everyone) program. Together, these additional services helped Tyler stay enrolled and engaged at LCA. He made many friends in the LIFE program and became popular among his peers.

Through all of his challenges, Tyler remained a diligent and successful student, ever committed to doing his very best. His passion to succeed was so strong that he would spend hours at home on his school work in order to keep pace with his classmates. Maintaining that level of achievement became increasingly difficult in direct correlation to the growing severity and aftereffects of the seizures.

From my office window on the third floor of the Buntain Learning Center, I could see Vickie bring Tyler and his sister, Jessica, to school each day. Their transportation was a minivan with sliding doors that allowed the easiest possible entry and exit. As he lost strength, Tyler moved into a wheelchair to increase his mobility and then began using a neck collar to support his head. Nevertheless, he continued to give his absolute best effort at all times, even as the seizures took their toll on his body, speech patterns, and memory.

By the end of eighth grade, Tyler's learning ability and body had been affected to the degree that he had difficulty maintaining regular enrollment. He was unable to maintain the pace of learning needed to remain enrolled at LCA. His parents decided to move him to a public school that could provide more services for students with learning and health challenges like Tyler's. Although he did not want to leave LCA, he applied every possible skill he had to do well in his new school. His efforts to succeed never diminished, and he made a positive impression on his peers at Clover Park High School. During his high school years, Tyler was voted king of the homecoming royal court—quite an achievement for a young man with so many challenges. Tyler never knew the word *quit*, and he battled to continue being and doing his very best.

Not long after graduating from high school, Tyler died in a drowning accident at his parents' lakeside home while experiencing a seizure. Only his death stopped him from continuing to learn and live the best life possible for a young man with such severe physical and mental challenges. To this day, his parents award the annual Tyler Saugen Memorial award to a LIFE program student who best exemplifies Tyler's determination and perseverance. This is one of LCA's most esteemed student achievement awards!

Tyler worked hard to be successful in all he did, including building valuable relationships with students and teachers. In 2016, several years after his death, his parents gave a significant gift to help Life Christian Academy undertake and complete a major remodel and retrofit of several classrooms to create the Tyler J. Saugen Success Center. This fantastic learning space includes new technology-loaded classrooms for the LIFE program, as well as a new media center and an innovation lab for use by all students. This facility, which has changed how education is delivered at Life Christian Academy, is a daily testament to the lifelong perseverance and continued influence of Tyler Saugen!

THE SIZE OF THE FIGHT IN THE PLAYER

Another of my favorite testimonials is the story of Dirk Kroeze, who was on the football team at North Dakota State University when I arrived in 1977 for my first season as a graduate assistant coach. One of my mentors on the NDSU coaching staff was Steve "Army" Armstrong, a fellow North Dakota native who had also been a graduate assistant before becoming a full-time assistant. Steve was on the path I hoped to take to becoming a college football coach. He told me the part of Dirk's story that had taken place before my arrival.

Dirk was from Williams, Minnesota, a small town near the Canadian border. He played high school football in a small program with limited exposure, but his goal was to play for the NDSU Bison. In the recruiting process, Dirk was passed over for bigger, faster players with better stats and stronger resumes, but he applied to NDSU and made contact with the football offices anyway. So head coach Jim Wacker sent Dirk a standard letter inviting him to a walk-on tryout with the team when school began, though the letter did not include an invitation to fall camp with the ninety or so players who were most likely to make the team.

Dirk did not accept that letter at face value. In August of his freshman year, on the same day the recruits all showed up, Dirk Kroeze walked down the hallway to the coaches' offices. None of the NDSU coaches recognized that determined young man. Coach Wacker invited Dirk into his office while he briefly reviewed the coaching staff's recruiting records. Sure enough, he found Dirk's name on the list of players who were supposed to report when school started. That list was a way to avoid paying to have second-tier athletes on the team for three weeks of fall camp. Once school was in session, the players were all on their regular room and board plan, so the football program saved money by not inviting players to camp who were unlikely to succeed.

When Coach Wacker asked Dirk if he had received the letter, Dirk acknowledged that he had. Then he went on to explain that he had saved up money for his meals and had a camper in the back of his pickup truck to sleep in. All he wanted was a chance to start practice at camp with the rest of the players. Jim Wacker was a master motivator of young men, and he could sense this young man was uncommonly determined. So he told Dirk to get his things, move into the dormitory with the rest of the players, and join the team for meals. Later that day, as the coaching staff walked from the athletic department offices to the food-service facility, they noticed an old pickup truck in the parking lot. They later learned that was the truck in which Dirk Kroeze had intended to sleep, and the "camper" to which he had referred was just a bedroll covered by a tarp! What was Dirk Kroeze willing to do to play at NDSU?

During his freshman year, Dirk was too small to play, so he was relegated to the scout squad, the group of players the varsity players got to beat on each day at practice. Dirk, however, was excited to be in any part of the program. He continued to improve, lift weights, get a bit larger, and work hard in practice on the scout squad. Watching Dirk's committed effort practice after practice, it became obvious to the coaches that he had an uncommon drive to succeed. Coach Wacker kept telling Army that he needed to look at this Kroeze kid.

In the off-season, Dirk worked hard in the weight room and did robust conditioning drills to prepare for spring football. He went through spring ball with his teammates, still on the small side but continuing to show progress, including overall agility and a quick first step off the ball as a defensive lineman. He was always eager to compete in practice, and he showed up in scrimmages against the varsity offense, often making plays that frustrated the starting units.

By the end of his redshirt freshman season, Dirk had gained fifteen pounds of muscle and earned playing time as a defensive lineman. His greatest assets were his quickness as a smaller-than-average defensive lineman and his keen instinct to find the ball. Dirk went on to lead the defensive unit at NDSU during his sophomore, junior, and senior years. He received the North Central Conference's most valuable player award and became a two-time All-American! Imagine the drive, determination, commitment, and perseverance that Dirk Kroeze—who earned the nickname "Crazy"—displayed over his years as a prolific Bison player. Uncommon in so many ways! How crazy is this story?

NEVER GIVE UP

I have great respect for entrepreneurs who show extreme levels of perseverance to ultimately realize their vision and dream. One of these is Josh Dunn, a young businessman whose first independent initiative was the establishment of a wedding events magazine for the South Puget Sound region. Unfortunately for Josh, the timing of his pursuit of funding for the magazine coincided with the terrorist attack on the Twin Towers in September of 2001, and the entire nation was grieving and unsettled.

Nevertheless, Josh continued to move toward his goal, contacting more than six hundred prospective businesses, including fifty-five that ultimately said yes to advertising in this new publication for the greater Tacoma area. The ratio of fifty-five affirmative responses to more than 550 negative ones means Josh had a 90 percent negative response rate in his quest to make the magazine a success. When I asked what kept him going, Josh replied, "I had to persevere. I was in a tough marketplace, but I believed in my product."

Josh also believed God would bring him the right staff, clients, and partners to make the effort successful, and this belief kept him focused on the positive. He didn't doubt that he was going to make his dream a reality. Four years after launching his wedding events magazine, Josh sold the business and used the proceeds to help launch a new venture. Today, 425 is the most successful business magazine for the Bellevue and Eastside neighborhoods of the greater Seattle area and a multimillion-dollar company—all from humble beginnings and great determination.

As I spoke with Josh about persevering, he said, "Most people are not willing to go the extra mile. Many get tired of being told no to an ask. For a different perspective, think about this: With every no I get, I'm closer to a yes. We have to be careful to know which voice we are listening to in life. So much of life is keeping on past the point when others quit."

Josh encourages entrepreneurs to establish boards of advisers to help them keep a balanced perspective and hold them accountable during times of challenge. These advisers also provide a ready source of wisdom and insight.

Nothing is more essential for success than the ability to stick to it. "People of mediocre ability," says Bernard Baruch, "sometimes achieve outstanding success because they don't know enough to quit." Thomas Edison once said that 75 percent of the world's failures wouldn't have failed at all if they'd only kept at what they were trying to do. "Our greatest weakness," he said, "lies in giving up. The most certain way to succeed is always to try just one more time."

PERSEVERANCE UNDER PRESSURE

I am blessed with great memories of my coaching days at Life Christian Academy—the players, coaches, games, and locker room celebrations. In athletics, a win is a win and a loss is a loss. We can learn from both, but we cherish most those wins that were hard fought and most difficult to attain.

In the 2006 postseason, our team was playing a quarterfinal state playoff game in late November. Our opponent was Adna, a strong program from southwest Washington, and the game was played on a neutral field at Tumwater High School. Ours was the first of two state playoff games played at Tumwater that day, so there was a festive atmosphere and excitement in the air.

I don't remember what I told our players before the game in my locker room speech. Whatever it was, it didn't work! In the first half, we fell significantly behind, and with five minutes remaining until halftime, Adna led by a score of 28–7. Adna had dominated the game, stopping our high-scoring spread offense and attacking our defense for four touchdowns in less than thirty minutes of play. Worse yet, they had driven the ball to our 5-yard line and were threatening to score their fifth touchdown of the first half. Our team seemed tentative, uncertain, and out of sync, but the Pirates never scored that touchdown from the 5-yard line. Instead, Eagle sophomore linebacker Morgan Cox made a big hit on an Adna ball carrier, forcing a fumble that senior defensive back Marcus Baldwin recovered.

Our offense then put together a 95-yard drive for a touchdown just before halftime, resulting in a 28–14 deficit to a very good and well-coached team. Our players still remember the pivotal moments of the game, including a halftime message of challenge and inspiration. We were down, but we were not done! That second-quarter fumble recovery and long scoring drive had slightly turned the momentum.

Our Eagle offense scored two touchdowns in the third quarter. Kicker Justin Peterson, who was battling the flu, remembers running on the field for the point after touchdown. He was nervous, but he made the kick for a 28–28 tie. We went on to score yet again in the fourth quarter for the go-ahead touchdown. Adna mounted one more drive late in the game, but Eagle junior nose guard Jon Donner intercepted an underthrown pass in our territory to stop the Pirates.

Had that been a different group of players, we might have lost the game. But that team knew how to persevere, keep battling, and come away with one of our school's all-time best wins. The players and LCA community still talk about the Adna game in 2006—and the 2007 state playoff game, which we also won.

As a leader, I have always believed that we learn much more about a person when the pressure is on than when the path is smooth. Whether in an athletic competition, health affliction, business downturn, or moral failure, a person's ability to overcome obstacles determines the outcome. Some people have the ability to persevere, whereas others do not. These lines of poetry are as applicable today as they were forty-three years ago when I first discovered them:

> How do you act when the pressure is on?
> When the chance for victory is almost gone,
> When fortune's star has refused to shine,
> When the ball is on your own five-yard line?
>
> How hard, how long will you fight the foe?
> That's what the world would like to know.
> Cowards can fight when they're out ahead;
> The uphill grind shows a thoroughbred![18]

KEEPING ON KEEPING ON

This chapter would not be complete without a few words about my friendship with Don Huber and his life story. Don was raised by a single mother, built his first home while attending college full-time, and has led a life of faith and perseverance for most of his eighty years. When I arrived in Tacoma in 1985, I had never heard of Don Huber, but I soon met him and learned that he had gone from building that first house to becoming one of the Pacific Northwest's largest real estate developers. Don later became an entrepreneur and inventor of unique products, which he continues to do today.

As I like to tease Don, eighty years is a long time to do anything, so God has clearly been on his side! During his life, Don has been confronted with challenges, just as we all have. He has persevered through difficult economic times, challenging family dynamics, new market conditions, and providing for a large family. During the 2008 economic crash, he went through bankruptcy and a difficult divorce. However, according to his son Dylan, Don never doubted that good days were ahead. He knew he would rebound, and his life has been a testimony to perseverance.

Don's faith, work ethic, and diligence has helped him "keep on keeping on." He has consistently rebounded from things that would have caused many people to quit. Because of his resolve to overcome and find a path forward, he has also become a significant encourager to many people, including his own children. Dylan indicated that time and again, Don's voice has been a voice of faith and confidence that his children are on the correct path. He is a cheerleader for other people, and if I want an encouraging word, I call Don—or even better, go see him!

This book is about the power of words spoken or written. Don's testimony of perseverance is also trademarked by his ability to encourage others. He and I have shared numerous board meetings, committee meetings, and personal conversations. Consistently and frequently, his voice is one of optimism, vision, and encouragement. We all need a Don Huber alongside us as an example of faith and perseverance. His life has been filled with both, and I am grateful for my friend Don.

SAYINGS

> Life is 10 percent what happens to you and 90 percent how you react to it.
> —Charles R. Swindoll, pastor and author, and Kris Diaz, Baldwin Wallace University

Adversity can knock you down, but it cannot keep you down if you won't let it.
—Mickey Andrews, Florida State University

There is no such thing as defeat, except when it comes from within. As long as a person doesn't admit he is defeated, he isn't. He's a little behind, but he isn't through fighting.
—Darrell Royal, University of Texas

Put your face in the cold north wind.
—Grant Teaff, Baylor University

You will not be remembered for what you do; you will be remembered for what you overcome.
—Jerry Moore, Appalachian State University

The trouble with most of us is that we stop trying in trying times.
—Denis Waitley, motivational speaker and consultant

Flush it and move on.
—Mark Venn, Lindbergh High School

Failure should be our teacher, not our undertaker. It should challenge us to new heights of accomplishment, not pull us to new depths of despair. Failure is delay, not defeat. It is a temporary detour, not a dead-end street.
—William Arthur Ward

Learn from mistakes; don't let them drag you down.
—Arthur Sanchez, Concrete High School

Bounce back.
—Johnny Watson, Little Rock Christian Academy

Everything worthwhile must be bought with sacrifice.
—Ara Parseghian, University of Notre Dame

Failure is not fatal, but failing to change might be.
—John Wooden, University of California, Los Angeles

Tough guys win.
—Eric Cohu, Little Rock Christian Academy

Tough times don't last; tough people do.
—Tim Camp, Eastern Oregon University

Let silence be your friend.
—Bill Alexander, Quincy High School

Will you be there when the grass turns green?
—Earl Carey Banks, Morgan State University, and his son
  Raymond Banks Sr.
  [Back in the 1960s, the regular football season for Morgan
  State would end after the Thanksgiving Classic with
  Virginia State College. By late November, the football field
  would be pretty chopped up and the grass virtually gone.
  Many players left school for various reasons at the end of
  the season. Coach Banks asked this question of his players,
  referring to the spring semester.]

Can you go when you are tired?
—Earl Carey Banks, Morgan State University

*I make my practices real hard, because if a player is a
quitter, I want him to quit in practice, not a game.*
—Paul "Bear" Bryant, University of Alabama

*Don't fear adversity, since facing it is the only way to
get stronger.*
—Unknown

Tape an aspirin on it.
—Grant Teaff, Baylor University

When things go wrong, don't ask, "Why me?" but instead say, "Try me."
—Phil Hayford, Keswick Christian School

I always told my team on game night, "No one in this locker room is going to play a perfect game tonight without any mistakes. There will always be room for something you could have done better. Your ability to learn and get over those mistakes will determine our success."
—Dick Zatkovich, Lincoln High School

After a loss, you have two choices: you can get better, or you can get bitter.
—Bobby Miller, Life Christian Academy

Before a game, I would remind our players that at some point in the game, bad things would happen. How you respond to adversity will determine what makes the difference in the outcome, and always remember: a setback is only an opportunity for a comeback.
—Sam McCorkle, Oxford High School

Play with pain—a must. Can't cater to injuries, especially the little ones.
—Tony Mason, University of Arizona

Rough neck, smooth back. Deal with adversity and let the bad stuff go.
—Benjamin Benavides III, John F. Kennedy High School

It's not the size of the dog in the fight that counts; it's the size of the fight in the dog.
—Bill Heglar, Interlake High School

NGU—never give up.
—Tom Sanchez, South Bend High School

A man doesn't stay defeated because of something that happened to him, but because of something that happened within him.
—Denis Isrow, North Dakota State University

That's why you have two of them.
—Dave Collins, Hope Community Church
  [In reference to someone injuring part of his body]

I can't get excited about losing a game. If we lose, we lose. It's part of the game and reality.
—Joe Paterno, Penn State University

Can you be comfortable being uncomfortable?
—Navy SEALS' mantra from Kirk Talley, Warner University

Never, never, never give up.
—Sid Otton, Tumwater High School

In adversity, there is opportunity.
—Bob Lucey, Curtis High School

Rub some dirt on it—applicable to pain.
—Steve Buuck, Faith Lutheran Middle School and High School

Adversity causes some men to break, others to break records.
—William Arthur Ward

Adversity only makes you stronger down the road.
—Janna Hjelseth, Tri-County High School

Keep on keeping on.
—Johnny Majors, University of Tennessee
—Mike Breeden, Heritage Christian Academy

QUESTIONS TO AFFECT YOUR LIFE

1) Describe the most adverse situation in your life.

2) What level of perseverance did you exhibit to overcome the adverse situation in question 1?

3) What can we learn from Josh Dunn's story of starting a business in a turbulent season and eventually becoming successful?

4) Who in your life has a life story similar to Tyler Saugen's journey?

HUMOR AND FUN

- The quality of being amusing or comic, especially as expressed in literature or speech
- The ability to express humor or make other people laugh
- Synonyms: comical aspect, comic side, funny side, comedy, funniness, hilarity, jocularity, absurdity, absurdness, ludicrousness, drollness, facetiousness, satire, irony; jokes, joking, jests, jesting, quips, witticisms, puns, wit, wittiness, comedy, jocularity, drollery, repartee, badinage, banter, raillery

In my early consideration of topics this book might address, I never envisioned a chapter on humor. However, as my inbox began to fill with responses to my invitation for memorable expressions or sayings, I noticed that several were funny and would evoke laughter in almost any situation. I began musing about the circumstances in which these may have been used by those who submitted them and reflecting on the unique role humor plays in our lives. Ultimately, I decided to add this chapter on the dynamics of humor and how, why, and when a funny line or anecdote adds value.

THE BEST MEDICINE

Humor is what happens when experiences or words provoke laughter and provide amusement. Whether accidental or intentional, humor can be both a form of entertainment and a means of coping with difficult or awkward situations and stressful events.

The word *humor* derives its roots from the humoral medicine of the ancient Greeks. According to the principles of this pathology, the balance of fluids in the human body, known as humours, controlled human health and emotions.

Expressions such as "He who laughs, lasts" and "Laughter is good for the soul" must have some degree of truth. After all, they have been passed down from generation to generation. I suspect many of the humorous sayings I received were submitted because the people who provided them felt they contributed something positive to the situations in which they were originally used.

In almost all cases, at least two parties participate where humor is present: the person who provides the humor, intentionally or unintentionally, and those who see or hear it. As with most things in life, when it comes to humor, context and timing are key. In instances where humor is intentional, the person who provides it feels it's a good time to lighten things up, relieve some stress, or brighten the mood within a group. Most of us can remember at least a few tense situations where a lighter moment was welcomed by all. The laughter that followed a funny anecdote, joke, or even an unwitting faux pas may have been just what was needed to take the edge off a stressful day or emotional time.

Also, I imagine many of us can think of a time when humor was created at our expense. Maybe it was a joke aimed at us or something we did that was unintentionally embarrassing. Perhaps our pride was too injured for us to join the laughter at the time, but it's been my observation that as we get further along in years, many of us take ourselves less seriously and better appreciate the lighter moments in life. As we mature, we are more able to laugh at ourselves and realize that we, too, can enjoy our most embarrassing moments.

FUN DOESN'T MAKE ITSELF

The synonyms for humor listed at the beginning of this chapter include words such as *comedy, funniness, hilarity, facetiousness, joking,* and *banter.* In a word: *fun.* As I look back at the various roles I have filled over the years, I know that being fun and creating fun have been key aspects of my journey.

Let's start with creating fun for myself. Though a handful of other people have significant influence, I am ultimately and solely responsible for how I choose to spend my time. If I'm not careful to approach my schedule with balance in mind, I can overload my calendar with issues and challenges that drain my energy, wear me down, and have me living on the edge with no margin for recharging.

What is the solution? Simply to ensure that fun is built into my schedule before the week ever begins. I'm not suggesting weekly vacations—just coffee with a friend, a lunch appointment with a former student or athlete, a morning walk with my dog, and so on. Such fun events provide the balance needed to offset the more taxing elements of work and life.

Having a healthy daily routine also helps cultivate a balanced life that includes fun. Activities such as study and prayer, journaling, exercise, and intentional gathering with friends help alleviate the day's tensions, as well as contribute to my physical and mental well-being. Although I am not a great golfer, an hour on the driving range or putting green also provides balance, fresh air, and perspective.

At the end of each week, as I plan for the next, I ask myself, *Was this a week of balance between work, play, achievement, and fun?* Life well lived is a function of consistently being able to answer "Yes" to that question.

THE COUPLE WHO PLAYS TOGETHER, STAYS TOGETHER

Next, there is creating fun with my wife, Ronni. I am a firm believer that continuing to date is essential long after the wedding vows. In any healthy, successful, long-term relationship, someone needs to exercise leadership for its character and pay it constant attention.

In my opinion, men should carry the responsibility for creating fun and building the marriage, one day at a time. I give this advice to my sons Brandon and Tyler, who are both now married and fathers to their own children.

Some people use the term *love language* to describe how we best receive care from others in a way that recharges us. Ronni has a strong affinity for fun. She never met a party or social setting she didn't like! I often tease her that she is having much more fun in life than I am. To her credit, she is very intentional about creating fun in her own life and the lives of others. If there is no party or laughter, just leave it to Ronni: she appreciates humor and fun. Don't we all?

When Ronni and I first married, I was coaching football at North Dakota State University. This meant long hours during the season, including at least three to four evenings in the office each week. When football season was over, recruiting season was even worse, because it meant being away from home a week at a time, only to return home for a weekend of recruiting activities. Being gone and arriving home late at night does not result in a healthy marriage!

To offset the hectic schedule, I came up with our weekly date night, which was time set aside just for Ronni and me. Date night meant things such as dinner at a nice restaurant, seeing a movie, spending time with another couple, or just getting an ice cream cone after a long drive around the neighborhood. The point of date night was to ensure that part of each week—on the schedule, so each of us could plan for it—was spent nurturing our relationship, showing our appreciation and care for each other, communicating about small and big items, and having fun together. Laughter and humor were almost always part of date nights.

The night of the week varied, but Thursday was the night most commonly set aside for Mom-and-Dad time. It was important that we had a budget to pay a babysitter, because with no sitter, there was no time for Ronni and me to work on our marriage.

TEAM TIME-OUT

For twenty-seven of my thirty-five years as a football coach, I was the head coach. Part of my responsibility was to provide fun for the coaching staff, their wives, the players, and the support staff in the program. It is easy for anything—even football—to become mundane, boring, and energy draining. Routine is often the enemy of spontaneity and fun.

I had several ways of creating fun for the coaching staff. Coaches work long hours, so surprising them with the announcement that we were changing the weekly schedule to include an extra night off with family was always met with a hoot and a holler! Meals with the staff and their families at our home were another means of creating a break in the schedule to talk, laugh, and enjoy life together.

I was also responsible for creating fun for the players. An occasional Popsicle break midway through a hot, grueling practice during fall camp or the extra season was always well received. I'd go to the grocery store and pick out just the right Popsicles for the team and coaches. Then I would tell the student manager just before practice that he needed to have a cooler ready with the Popsicles before blowing the air horn to signal a break. After the air horn blew, I would loudly announce, "Popsicle time!" The response was always enthusiastic. Besides the emotional lift it gave the team, there was another benefit as well. At the end of the break, we required each player to promptly put his wrapper in the garbage can, which was a small lesson in building character. Anybody can leave a mess behind, but responsible people leave an area better for those who will use it later.

Another way to break up the routine of a football program was to schedule a bowling or movie night. College football players are athletic, but this does not necessarily mean they are successful bowlers. Two hours of team bowling at an alley near campus yielded a multitude of laughs and a lot of fun with one another. One of the benefits of bowling night was that the players interacted with others with whom they didn't normally engage during daily practice. For example, bowling provided the opportunity for players on offense, defense, or special teams to interact with and enjoy one another. What laughter and fun filled the bowling alley!

The same was true with team movie night. Instead of meeting in our regular classroom meeting areas, we would reserve a different campus facility, choose a movie, and have the entire team and coaching staff attend. We showed everything from NFL highlight films to emotional movies. One evening during fall camp at North Dakota State University, we watched *The Longest Day*. Popcorn and soda were also a part of movie night. At the University of Puget Sound, the tradition for almost fifty years was "corn and dew," which referred to movie night for the football team with popcorn and Mountain Dew.

Were these activities extra work, and did they require extra planning? Of course, but the effort was well worth it. Again, the point was to be intentional in scheduling fun into the week or season.

ON-THE-JOB FUN

Lastly, workplaces that have fun together are workplaces and organizations that last. Although the best leaders may be demanding and driven, they can also provide a fun workplace culture. For me, this included recognition of birthdays and regularly scheduled all-staff functions with minimal agendas, snacks, and time for laughter and social conversation. Never underestimate the power of providing relaxation and fun for your team members and employees. Treating your employees to a local baseball game, a barbecue at your home, or an afternoon at a community park with a picnic and games are all ways of "filling the tank" of your most valuable asset. Including spouses or family members is particularly beneficial.

Sometimes the little things are most significant when it comes to fun and appreciation. Think of the amount of time employees spend in meetings. I always felt that an effective meeting meant providing an agenda, a room prepped in advance, and a snack. Little details send a message that preparation is important and that your team members are important enough to prepare for.

I also enjoyed providing a surprise snack for employees or team members. Often this meant an early morning drive to our local Krispy Kreme. I would place an order for several dozen doughnuts the day before, and then pick them up and deliver them to the workplace before the 7:30 a.m. arrival of most staff. This small errand was fun for me, knowing that with a simple gesture, I could show appreciation for others' efforts, change the routine, and provide a sweet treat. Never did I encounter an employee on a Krispy Kreme day who wasn't thankful for the little lift of fun that a doughnut can provide!

Once a year at Life Christian Academy, with hundreds of students, staff, and parents on campus at the end of a school day, I would host an unscheduled free hot dog barbecue in one of the large common spaces adjacent to the parking lot and drive-through loop where parents picked up and dropped off their students. It was fun to see parents park and get out of their cars or students leave their hallway lockers and sprint to get a hot dog.

I mentioned having all-staff meetings on a regular basis. One often taken-for-granted "fun" element of a workplace is keeping employees informed. Everyone wants the scoop about what's going on! Sending an email is a means to an end, but think of the thousands of emails we all get. It's hardly a fun way to communicate.

One of my favorite all-staff meetings was planned by our administrative team with an extra dose of fun for everyone, including our leaders over the various aspects of our school. We created a news broadcast set with an anchor desk and backdrop. When the more than one hundred employees had taken their seats in the meeting room, the *LCA News* team walked out and took their positions behind the news desk. Our executive and administrative team members, dressed as news anchors and correspondents, had prepared scripts to share the news about LCA students, staff, and community. Instead of a boring presentation, team members delivered their news and commentary with fun and humor. We even created commercials. All in all, this was one of the most fun and memorable staff meetings in my twenty-six years as head of school. Again, lots of laughter!

FINISHING WITH FUN

Do you believe finishing well is important, whether finishing the day, an event, or a project? And if so, how do you determine what it looks like to finish well, and then make sure it happens?

In my coaching career, I quickly learned that the general feeling shared by the team at the end of a practice or game could be either pride, when they felt they had performed well, or discouragement and frustration, if they knew they hadn't done well. Over time, I realized that an important part of my role was to help direct these feelings toward "finishing well."

As I mentioned earlier, we used "'attaways" to encourage players and coaches to recognize those who had a great practice, play, or week. We would gather our entire team together at the end of every practice and open the floor for any player or coach to acknowledge someone who had gone above and beyond. After each affirmation, we did a brief team chant and clap to honor the player being recognized. In this way, we wrapped up each practice by rallying together and recalling its high points, rather than focusing on the negative or simply allowing players and coaches to walk off the field. This regular exercise helped build morale, because everyone enjoys being recognized and affirmed. And in addition to going our separate ways in a positive frame of mind, together we learned the life lesson that it is fun to recognize others for their achievements.

On game days, both at home and away, we integrated this tradition into the postgame routine. We rallied our team at the end of the stadium grandstand, including the parents and fans, and did the same "'attaway" chant and clapping for all. This was especially fun to do at games on the road, as the other teams' fans observed our "'attaway" time on their field. It was a powerful affirmation that there was more to the outcome than the numbers on the scoreboard—another important timeless lesson!

THE LESSON

In my second full year as the head of a Christian school, I received a brief parody from my friend Rich Wilkerson, an evangelist whose four boys attended our school. The humorous message it conveyed was that even Jesus encountered challenges when it came to students' reactions to His teaching.

> Then Jesus took his disciples up the mountain, and gathering them around him, He taught them, saying: "Blessed are the poor in spirit, for theirs is the kingdom of Heaven. Blessed are the meek. Blessed are they that mourn. Blessed are the merciful. Blessed are they that thirst for justice. Blessed are you when you are persecuted. Blessed are you when you when you suffer. Be glad and rejoice for your reward is great in heaven."
>
> Then Simon Peter said, "Do we have to write this down?"
>
> Then Andrew asked, "Are we supposed to know this?"
>
> And James asked, "Will we be tested on this?"
>
> And Phillip said, "I don't have any paper."
>
> And Bartholomew asked, "Do we have to turn this in?"
>
> And John said, "The other disciples don't have to learn this."
>
> And Matthew asked, "Can I go to the bathroom?"
>
> And Judas asked, "What does this have to do with real life?"
>
> Then one of the Pharisees who was present asked to see Jesus's lesson plan and inquired of Jesus, "Where is your anticipatory set? Are your objectives in the cognitive domain?"
>
> And Jesus wept!

SCHOOL VOICEMAIL PHONE RESPONSES

The following was sent to me in 2000 by one of my teachers, Stan Seely.

> You have reached the automated answering service for your school. To assist you in connecting to the right staff member, please listen to all the options before making a selection:
>
> - To lie about why your child is absent, press 1.
> - To make excuses for why your child did not do his work, press 2.
> - To complain about what we do, press 3.
> - To cuss out staff members, press 4.
> - To ask why you didn't get information that was in your newsletter and several bulletins mailed to you, press 5.
> - If you want us to raise your child, press 6.
> - If you want to reach out and touch, slap, or hit someone, press 7.
> - To request another teacher for the third time this year, press 8.
> - To complain about bus transportation, press 9.
> - To complain about school lunches, press 10.
> - If you realize this is the real world and your child must be accountable/responsible for his/her own behavior, classwork, homework, and that it's not the teachers' fault for your child(ren)'s lack of effort, *hang up and have a nice day!*

CLASSIC EXCUSES

Another favorite source of school-related humor is the ongoing anthology of written excuses submitted by parents explaining their child's absence or failure to complete a homework assignment. I was given this list by a colleague several years ago:

- My son is under a doctor's care and should not take P. E. today. Please execute him.
- Please excuse Lisa for being absent. She was sick, and I had her shot.
- Dear School, please excuse John being absent on January 28, 29, 30, 31, 32, and also 33.
- Please excuse Roland from P. E. for a few days. Yesterday he fell out of a tree and misplaced his hip.
- John has been absent because he had two teeth taken out of his face.
- Megan could not come to school today because she has been bothered by very close veins.
- Chris will not be in school because he has an acre in his side.
- Please excuse Jimmy for being. It was his father's fault.
- Please excuse Jennifer for missing school yesterday. We forgot to get the Sunday paper off the porch, and when we found it on Monday, we thought it was Sunday.
- Sally won't be in school a week from Friday. We have to attend her funeral.

NORTH DAKOTA

Last but not least, Jeff Foxworthy has entertained thousands with his comedy and humorous presentations. Since I am from North Dakota, I thought I would conclude this chapter with a selection of Foxworthy's only slightly exaggerated statements about my home state:

- If you consider it a sport to gather your food by drilling through eighteen inches of ice and sitting there all day hoping that the food will swim by, you might live in North Dakota.
- If your local Dairy Queen is closed from November through March, you might live in North Dakota.

- If you instinctively walk like a penguin for five months out of the year, you might live in North Dakota.
- If your dad's suntan stops at a line curving around the middle of his forehead, you might live in North Dakota.
- If you have had a lengthy telephone conversation with someone who dialed the wrong number, you might live in North Dakota.
- If your town has an equal number of bars and churches, you might live in North Dakota.
- If the Fourth of July community picnic was moved indoors due to frost, you might live in North Dakota.
- If you have more miles on your snow blower than your car, you might live in North Dakota.
- If you design your child's Halloween costume to fit over a snowsuit, you might live in North Dakota.

As I look back on my various seasons and circles of community, I remember well the people who consistently carried laughter with them everywhere they went. It's almost impossible for me to think of them without smiling.

Life is long and short, difficult and fun, costly and rewarding. I encourage you to make time to see, share, create, and enjoy the humor and laughter! And appreciate the people in your life who give the gift of fun.

SAYINGS

If lessons are learned in defeat, our team is getting a great education.
—Murray Warmath, University of Minnesota

It's kind of hard to rally around a math class.
—Paul "Bear" Bryant, University of Alabama

This is the greatest country in America.
—Phil Hayford, Keswick Christian School

Halftime scores are the most overrated statistic in football.
—Mike Van Diest, Carroll College

The hay is never in the barn.
—Mike Van Diest, Carroll College

There is a special place in heaven for football coaches' wives.
—Phil Hayford, Keswick Christian School

Running is fun. Fun is running. Now get your butt moving.
—Tom Merrill, John F. Kennedy High School

Our team this year will not be big but will be slow.
—Unknown

We tried to implant college into him, and his body rejected it.
—Barry Switzer, University of Oklahoma (on why he had to drop a player from the squad)

Howard Cosell has been announcing football games for years—though not necessarily the one he is watching.
—Milton Berle

Undertakers aren't bad guys. They're just the last ones to let you down.
—Unknown

He's pretty clumsy. I once saw him spill Vaseline.
—Unknown

We were tipping off our plays every time we broke the huddle. Three backs were laughing and one was as pale as a ghost.
—John Breen, Houston Oilers (after quitting the team)

Pain is in your head, injury is in a cast, an owie is nothing. Now, show me your cast.
—Tom Merrill, John F. Kennedy High School

God can't steer a parked car.
—Jud Keim, Pacific Lutheran University

We're not going to throw a parade for you.
—Steve Cain, University of Puget Sound

He is as tough as a nickel steak.
—Scott Smith, Legacy Christian Academy

After having dinner with several of us ballplayers, Tommy Lasorda would be told by the restaurant manager that he had a phone call (which he had previously arranged with the manager). Then he would get up to take the call and never show up again—which left us players to pay the bill.
—Bill Ralston on Tommy Lasorda, manager of the Los Angeles Dodgers

Ralston was voted the second-best looking guy on the team. Everyone else tied for first.
—Tommy Lasorda on Bill Ralston

This team has many highly educated men. Ralston has a PhD—a posthole digger degree. Zahn has a CPA—cleaning, pressing, and alterations degree.
—Tommy Lasorda on his players

Coulda, woulda, shoulda. If he, and yeah but, too.
—Dave Nelson, Minnetonka High School

If ifs and buts were candy and nuts, we would all have a party.
—Paul Wallrof, University of Puget Sound

It ain't so much what you know, but what you think you know that just ain't so.
—Jim Christopherson, Concordia University, Minnesota

Pull your head out of your butt.
—Buck Nystrom, Michigan State University

Stupidity is terminal.
—Grant Teaff, Baylor University

Can't never did anything.
—Grant Teaff, Baylor University

All I want to see moving is your elbow and your butthole.
—Fred Manuel, Lane College

I see some good things, and I see some not good things.
—Fred Manuel, Lane College

Flush it and move on.
—Mark Venn, Lindbergh High School

All else being equal, I'll take luck over skill.
—Bill Kiefer, Wahpeton High School

I can't wait till tomorrow, because you get better looking every day.
—Larry Prather, Reinhardt University

If a dog will bite, he will bite as a pup.
—John Cooper, Ohio State University

I am going to smoke your lamps.
—Mike Anderson, University of Wisconsin lacrosse

Skin is waterproof.
—Courtney Meyer, Concordia University, Nebraska

Dig, dig, little pig. Root or die, the best man wins.
—Larry Kindbom, Washington University

Some dogs just won't hunt.
—Jovan Hayne, Vanderbilt University

Are you truly happy or just having fun?
—Tim Camp, Eastern Oregon University

Are your ears painted on?
—Bill Alexander, Quincy High School

When all is said and done, more is said than done.
—Aesop, and Lou Holtz, College of William and Mary

Stand on your helmet and put the sideline under your armpit for the national anthem.
—Paul Wallrof, University of Puget Sound

QUESTIONS TO AFFECT YOUR LIFE

1) Who do you appreciate for their humor, laughter, frolic, and fun?

2) How can you tell when your life is out of balance or lacking margin?

3) What is your favorite fun thing to do that you need regularly?

4) Assignment: Schedule the week ahead with your perfect balance of work, responsibility, humor, and fun. Stick to the schedule, and at the end of the week, evaluate what you created. Your schedule becomes your reality and your life well lived.

LEADERSHIP

- The action of leading a group of people or an organization
- The state or position of being a leader
- Synonyms: guidance, direction, authority, control, management, superintendence, supervision; headship, directorship, administration, jurisdiction, captaincy, mastery, command, power, domination, rule, governance
- According to the idea of transformational leadership, an effective leader is a person who does the following: creates an inspiring vision for the future, motivates and inspires people to engage with that vision, manages delivery of the vision, and coaches and builds a team so it is more effective at achieving the vision. Leadership brings together the skills needed to do these things.[19]
- Qualities of a good leader: honesty and integrity, confidence, ability to inspire others, commitment and passion, good communicator, decision-making capabilities, accountability, delegation and empowerment, creativity and innovation, empathy[20]

Leadership is not easy at any age or in any assignment. Effective leadership requires vision, wisdom, discernment, decision making, communication, confidence, and follow-through. Leadership does not depend on a person's title; leaders can and do emerge at any level.

Thus far in my life, I have found myself leading in contexts ranging from choosing teams at recess as an elementary student to serving as a head football coach for more than a quarter of a century, serving as president of several organizations, leading our family alongside my wife, and creating and leading a school for twenty-six years. Most recently, I have founded Hjelseth and Associates, LLC, a consulting and coaching business to assist leaders and their organizations. In each of these roles, I have sought out and endeavored to make the most of opportunities to learn from other people. Continuous leaders are continuous learners.

IN WORD AND DEED

Leadership often takes the form of verbal exhortation and/or setting an example through action. Timely words from a perceived leader can inspire other people and have a significant effect on them. Likewise, a leader's compelling example can propel others toward commitment, inspiration, and diligence in the direction of accomplishing a goal or realizing a vision. Both verbal and exampled leadership are part of most leaders' influence on their people. Coaches who inspire their teams with pointed pregame locker room speeches, combined with players' observance of and familiarity with their coach's example, puts a stamp of inspiration, energy, and focus on any team's efforts during a game.

My University of Puget Sound football team entered the 1987 season with just six seniors on the roster. Those six had been on the 1985 and 1986 teams, both of which finished second in our division of the Columbia Football League. In each of those seasons, the Loggers had won every home game but lost a key game on the road, which had kept them out of the NAIA national playoffs. In other words, we had been close, but no cigar!

In the months leading up to the 1987 season, I met regularly with these six seniors to discuss improvements, leadership, and goals. In every discussion, we talked about the need to win on the road. The season began with a high-energy fall camp that was scheduled to culminate in a season-opening game in the Tacoma Dome against Pacific Lutheran University, played for our season's largest crowd in the city's largest venue. We would be playing that game, which we had lost the previous two years, away from our home field of Baker Stadium.

The week leading up to the game was fun and charged with energy. Anticipation for the season was in the air, the food, our practices, and the meeting rooms. On game day, we shared our traditional pregame meal at 2:30 p.m., held our usual meetings in the athletic department, and then headed to the buses for the thirty-minute drive to the game site. As usual, I took roll as each player stepped onto the bus. Last to board was Mike Oliphant, our senior captain and returning All-American running back.

Upon arriving at the Dome, we went through pregame warmups. With twenty minutes remaining until kickoff, our team headed to the locker rooms for final game preparations. As I walked with our assistant coaches down the hallway, we heard a lot of noise coming from the locker room. That was atypical, for such noise usually came after—rather than before—our pregame talk. As the assistant coaches and I looked at one another, we knew our guys were ready to play.

When we walked into the locker room, there was sod and dirt all over the players' uniforms and on the floor. Where had the sod come from? Mike Oliphant had smuggled a large garbage sack of sod from our home practice fields into his team travel bag. He had left the pregame warm-ups a bit early to be the first one back to the Tacoma Dome locker rooms. As his teammates came in, Mike had rubbed sod and dirt into their white game uniforms. His message to them was "We are on the Baker bog. This is our field!"

That night we dominated the game, winning 24–7, and Mike scored three touchdowns to lead his Logger teammates to a great win. Our postgame locker room time was an enthusiastic celebration and appreciation for Mike's sack of "Baker bog," which had reminded us to play as if we were on our own field. The 1987 team remained undefeated, winning road games with a sack of Baker field sod making every trip. Unfortunately Mike sustained a season-ending dislocated hip in game seven, and with that, our team lost a home game.

Mike's leadership, both verbal and exampled, helped prepare his team for a better season in which we would win on the road. Mission accomplished! Mike went on to play four seasons with the Washington Redskins and Cleveland Browns—not bad for a young man who never played high school football!

LEADING BY SERVING

I was born in 1951, and my earliest ideas about leadership were heavily influenced by the top-down dynamic prevalent during my formative years. It was a widely accepted practice for leaders to use their authority to tell their subordinates how to serve the organization, and subordinates were expected to show respect for their leaders. Roles such as president, CEO, colonel, superintendent, elected official, head coach, and so on have long been esteemed simply for their status.

Over the past few decades, however, the idea of leading by serving others has gained credibility and acceptance throughout Western culture. Defining leadership on the basis of hierarchy and title is increasingly perceived as oudated and ineffective.

Servant leadership is distinctive in both implementation and outcomes. Servant leaders perceive their role as follower and learner first, then servant, and finally leader. Unlike leadership models in which levels of administration separate leaders from entry-level participants, servant leaders make a marked effort to be close to people whom they lead and aware of their needs. Servant leaders know that they must be with people in order to know how to best serve them. Conversely, leaders who are distant from their people lose touch with them. Leaders who spend time among those they are leading (and serving) not only gain valuable knowledge, but also earn and build invaluable relationship and trust—two elements that heavily influence the effectiveness of a leader and the success of the endeavor being led.

Jesus, arguably the greatest leader of all time, articulated serving as His highest priority. In Matthew 20:28, He said that He "did not come to be served, but to serve" (NIV).

In addition to being present and accessible, servant leaders pursue intentional, two-way communication with people at all levels of the organization or team, so that every member understands the mission, vision, and significance of their individual and shared roles and objectives. A shared vision has a much stronger presence in organizations that have embraced a servant leadership culture than within those that subscribe to a hierarchical paradigm. A true servant leadership culture is marked by significant transparency in the circulation of information, goals, data, and results. Ultimately, servant leadership engages more people and elevates outcomes, because employees, team members, and volunteers feel informed, listened to, and cared about. All of this, in turn, produces greater ownership and investment at every level.

CLEAR COMMITMENT

In his book titled *Start with Why: How Great Leaders Inspire Everyone to Take Action*, Simon Sinek asserts that the most influential leaders begin by consistently and effectively answering the question "Why?" He goes on to detail illustration after illustration of this premise, including the Wright brothers' quest to fly their airplane, the passion of Steve Jobs and Andrew Wozniak to create the personal computer, and Dr. Martin Luther King Jr.'s commitment to gaining freedom for people of all ethnicities.

Sinek's most vivid example of leadership and resilience under pressure is the story of Ernest Shackleton, an English adventurer who set out with twenty-seven men to explore the Antarctic. He and his crew embarked in December 1914 on the *Endurance*, a 320-ton ship, to travel seventeen hundred miles to the South Pole. However, mere days after setting sail, the ship was surrounded by ice jams and soon frozen in place in the South Atlantic. Shackleton and his crew were stuck in the ice for ten months, until the pressure of the ice finally crushed the *Endurance*. On November 21, 1915, the ship sank as the crew watched from the ice. Shackleton then ordered everyone to board three lifeboats and they made their way to tiny Elephant Island. There Shackleton left twenty-two of his crew while he and five others traveled eight hundred miles of rough seas to find help.

What makes the story of the *Endurance* remarkable is that no one died, there was no mutiny, and there are no stories of people eating their dead comrades. That had nothing to do with luck, but everything to do with the crew Shackleton had hired. How had he found the right men for the job? With a simple advertisement in the *London Times*: "Men wanted for hazardous journey. Small wages, bitter cold, long months of complete darkness, constant danger, safe return doubtful. Honor and recognition in case of success." Those who applied had understood the challenge and believed in the "why" of the journey.[21]

THE TRUSTWORTHY LEADER

Several qualities of a leader are listed at the beginning of this chapter. In my experience, developing trust is a key aspect of the leader's journey and critical to any hope of sustained leadership. Effective leaders are adept at earning and building trust with the people around them. Day in and day out, they must engage the discipline needed to maintain the highest level of honesty, integrity, humility, and worthiness of the trust placed in them. Leaders who earnestly pursue this standard can be trusted to consistently do the right thing.

Each of us can recall examples of people who led for decades because people knew they could be trusted at every turn. The evangelist Billy Graham and missionary Mother Teresa are two Greatest Generation examples of longtime leaders who continuously portrayed integrity and honesty in their efforts to serve people. They received high marks as trustworthy leaders.

On the flip side, most of us can also vividly remember leaders whose lack of integrity in a single instance broke the trust barrier.

In almost any category—sports, entertainment, religion, politics, corporate, nonprofit—a significant number of high-profile leaders have "flamed out" after betrayal of one type or another, including financial dishonesty, embezzlement, moral failure, underhanded dealings with people, and so on.

Today's culture is trust deficient, and not without cause. People are constantly evaluating the commitment and character of a veteran or aspiring leader. Any error interpreted as questionable, or that scatters seeds of doubt, tears at the fabric of trust. And when leaders betray trust, people are quick to dismiss their ability to lead, which nudges the stakes for leading with integrity, honesty, humility, and wisdom higher than ever.

LEADERSHIP IN ADVERSITY

When stock market indexes are high, profits are up, or a team has a two-goal lead in a soccer match with a minute to play, a leader's best leadership abilities are not really tested. Real leaders are most apparent when market conditions are tough, sales are down, a chronic illness sets in, or a team is behind by a touchdown with three minutes to play in the fourth quarter. True character and ability come to the surface when the going gets tough!

Ten Minutes on the Clock

In 1985, in my first season as head coach at the University of Puget Sound, our team had a 6–2 win-loss record heading into our last regular-season game. The game was played against Whitworth College on our home field at Baker Stadium on a sunny cold day in mid-November. Although our team had the best record, Whitworth played and coached better for most of the game. In fact, with approximately ten minutes to play in the fourth quarter, our Logger team trailed the Pirates by 28–7. We were facing what appeared to be an impossible uphill climb to pull out a win, which might allow us to make it to the NAIA national playoffs.

Suddenly we scored a touchdown, putting us within two touchdowns of victory. Optimism began to show in the eyes of our players. Then our defense forced a turnover, our offense scored again, and the twenty-one-point deficit was reduced to seven. Whitworth had the ball and the opportunity to kill much of the clock, but their quarterback was unable to sustain a drive, throwing incomplete passes that did little to run out the clock. Hope and determination burned in our players' eyes.

A short time later, to our home crowd's delight, our offense scored another touchdown and our kicker successfully kicked the extra point for a 28–28 tie with less than two minutes to go. Our sideline erupted with energy. Our kickoff team snuffed out any hope of a decent return by the Pirates, and with less than a minute of play remaining, our defense intercepted an overthrown pass in Pirate territory. With everyone on their feet, our offensive line opened holes, protected our quarterback, and led us to our fourth touchdown in less than ten minutes. Final score: UPS 35, Whitworth 27. What a momentous come-from-behind victory! But more importantly, what a testimony to effective team leadership when confronted with adversity!

That team will always remember that win. And when I get to heaven, I will still fondly remember those ten minutes.

EIGHT MONTHS TO LIVE

I have personally seen a handful of people model exceptional leadership while facing extremely difficult life circumstances. One was my dear friend and colleague Bobb Absten, who served on my administrative team at Life Christian Academy for nine years as high school principal. I hired Bobb, formerly a pastor in our Tacoma community, to lead and shepherd our high school student body. I felt our high school students and families needed his loving, affirming influence in their lives. Bobb brought all this to our school community—and much, much more.

In December 2011, Bobb began to experience indigestion, but thinking it was merely the flu, he continued his diligent and faithful service to our students, families, faculty, and staff until Christmas vacation. In early January, I received a phone call from Bobb, who had undergone testing to find out why he continued to have a "bad stomach." The test results were starkly conclusive. Bobb had stage 4 pancreatic cancer with a prognosis of four to six months to live.

Our entire Life Christian Academy community was shaken by this news. But Bobb, a man of steadfast faith in Jesus and personal willpower, continued his work at our school throughout chemotherapy and radiation treatments, hospital stays to regain strength, and ongoing fatigue. He never wavered in his belief that he was going to beat cancer. As much as he was able, Bobb was present at work and would hear nothing of taking time off. His commitment to leading was honorable.

In late May, Bobb was released from the hospital to finish the school year. To this day, people remember his inspiring, emotional speech to Life Christian Academy's graduating senior class of 2012. Just two months later, on August 4, surrounded by his wife, Juli, and their five children, Bobb took his last breath on earth and "graduated" to heaven. He was the consummate leader to the end.

This journey alongside Bobb tested my own leadership as well. As head of school, my role included encouraging and comforting students, staff, and families during those eight months and well beyond. As I look back, I can see God's faithfulness in giving me the right thoughts, words, and actions for our community just when they needed them. He was also a daily source of wisdom and guidance for me, as well as comfort in my own grief and loss of a treasured colleague and friend.

To honor Bobb's greatly missed leadership and presence at Life Christian Academy, I did not hire a high school principal for the following school year. Instead, the executive team and I partnered closely to collectively fulfill those responsibilities while we took time to thoughtfully seek the next leader for the role Bobb had filled so well. Years later, Bobb's leadership continues to influence the lives of LCA students, families, faculty, and staff through the unique culture he helped shape and build. Likewise, his leadership influence continues in the lives of those he once mentored as high school students, who have now become professionals, parents, and leaders themselves.

SEVENTY DAYS WITHOUT DAYLIGHT

Recently I came across the inspiring story of Luis Urzúa, a fifty-four-year-old shift foreman at the San José mine in Chile. On August 5, 2010, his crew of thirty-three men were trapped seven hundred meters underground by a collapse at the mine.

According to reports published in *The Guardian* during and after the rescue, Urzúa immediately began leading with authority. He established rules, schedules, and assignments for everything from food rationing and map making to sleeping, daylight simulation (using the headlights of mining trucks), sanitation, and letter writing. Seventeen days after the collapse, when rescue crews finally succeeded in drilling a hole all the way down to the miners, all were alive though none had eaten in forty-eight hours.

The Chilean government devised three possible evacuation plans, each of which depended on Urzúa and his team accomplishing specific tasks within the mine to ensure success. The result? Seventy days after the collapse, Urzúa was the last to ascend to daylight after the successful rescue of all his men. "You just have to speak the truth and believe in democracy," he explained when asked how he had kept his crew focused and alive.[22]

What a true test of unwavering leadership by Luis Urzúa!

CALLED TO LEAD

The path to leadership does not often follow a planned sequence of steps or training schedule. In my conversations with several leaders, I found that their abilities and roles were shaped over time. No two had followed the same path to leadership.

Tyler Sollie, a 1998 graduate of Life Christian Academy and now the lead pastor at Life Center church, describes his pastoral leadership role as a "calling" on his life. Tyler says he knew at a young age that his life was to be defined by ministry. Referring to some of the challenges of his current role, he said, "A leader has to be willing to manage ambiguity." In other words, a leader must lead in the midst of a storm of issues or events. During these times, Tyler says, a sense of being called helps keep the leader moving forward. This sense of purpose and passion asserts its presence in challenge and adversity.

Pastor Sollie also talked about the role of leaders in influencing their inner circle of staff. The essence of good leadership is leading by developing others. This doesn't happen by accident, but instead with intentional observation, listening, mentoring, and guidance. Leaders must spend time with those on whose support they depend and with whom they are partnering. If they are being led well, those closest to the leader should be able to demonstrate their teachings and example.

LEADING WITH HEART

How does leadership present itself to others? Mike Colbrese, former executive director of the Washington Interscholastic Activities Association, answers this question with a smile. When he walks into an appointment or meeting, whether with a small group of people or a large audience, his smile and high energy say a lot before he actually speaks. His administrative assistant, Chi Chi Bruskland, used to remind the WIAA staff to smile when they answered the phone. This was her way of encouraging the entire team to extend warmth, caring, and listening attitudes to people they served each day.

Mike also addressed the role of leadership in choosing and aligning staff members for optimum success. Knowing the strengths and weaknesses of team members helps make the most of their strengths, but also presents opportunities to strengthen areas of weakness. The best organizations have the best people performing at their best levels, but also help those people become even better.

As a result, the organization provides the best possible service to its customers or clients.

Another aspect of leadership Mike referenced was inviting his staff to challenge him on issues. He acknowledged that in many cases, other staff members are closer to an issue than he is and may have a better solution; at a minimum, they have valuable perspectives worth considering. Although it is understood by all that Mike has ultimate decision-making authority, he tries not to dictate a solution without first listening to the voices of his team. He hired them, invests in them, and believes in listening to them.

LEADERS ON LEADERSHIP

John Ralston spent a career in leadership as a head football coach at collegiate and professional levels. At a coaches' clinic in the late 1970s, I listened to John articulate three characteristics of professionals:

1. They love what they're doing in life.
2. They recognize that they have a responsibility to improve every day (school is never out; a leader is always learning).
3. They learn to set personal standards far beyond what is expected of them by others.

When I took these notes, I was a young head coach and teacher at a small school in Powers Lake, North Dakota. Little did I know how much these characteristics would shape my life in leadership.

Dwight D. Eisenhower, who spent a career in leadership before and after being elected president of the United States, saw leadership as a standard that not everyone could meet. He developed a list of five types of people who are unsuited for high command:

1. The self-seeking in matters of promotion
2. Those who try to pass the buck
3. Those who try to do everything

4. Those who shout or pound on desks because they yearn for the limelight
5. Pessimists who see the negative in situations[23]

Theodore Roosevelt, twenty-sixth president of the United States (1901–1909), is renowned for his authorship of an inspirational piece called "The Man in the Arena":

> It is not the critic who counts; not the man who points out how the strong man stumbles, or where the doer of deeds could have done them better. The credit belongs to the man who is actually in the arena, whose face is marred by dust and sweat and blood; who strives valiantly; who errs, who comes short again and again, because there is no effort without error and shortcoming; but who does actually strive to do the deeds; who knows great enthusiasms, the great devotions; who spends himself in a worthy cause; who at the best knows in the end the triumph of high achievement, and who at the worst, if he fails, at least fails while daring greatly, so that his place shall never be with those cold and timid souls who neither know victory nor defeat.[24]

I believe that leadership defines the world and creates change in a world needing improvement. The leader may be scorned for failure or challenge unmet, but he will always know he has tried his best. As I used to tell my players, "Do your best; God will do the rest."

SAYINGS

When the national anthem is played, I talk to myself and say, "Keep it simple, stupid. Don't get complicated. You can only give them what they can absorb."
—Al McGuire, Marquette University

Tuck the ball up and high, just like your goals.
—Arthur Sanchez, Concrete High School

It's not how many times you hit, get hit, or score that matters, but how you respond to those pivotal moments of pressure.
—Gus Martin, Life Christian Academy

Only the best can do the tough stuff, and the cream of the crop can do it even under excruciating pressure.
—Gus Martin, Life Christian Academy

All it takes is all you got.
—Johnny Tusa, Waco High School

Aggressive leadership is priceless.
—Vince Lombardi, Green Bay Packers

Do something today that your future self will thank you for.
—Mike Breeden, Heritage Christian Academy

Don't worry about the horse going blind; just lead the wagon and pull the line.
—John Cooper, Ohio State University

Poise under pressure.
—Bill Diedrick, high school and college coach

What makes a losing coach stay in the coaching profession? Perhaps a push from God, or a little freckle-faced boy in dirty tennis shoes, or maybe just a dream of how it might be sometime soon.
—Richard L. Hardy

As a coach, you must have no indecision. None.
—Al McGuire, Marquette University

MAD—Make a difference. Have an impact always.
—John Stiegelmeier, South Dakota State University

Your actions speak so loudly, I can't hear what you are saying.
—Bobby Hauck, University of Montana

Your actions speak so loudly, I can barely hear what you are saying.
—Pat Hill, Fresno State University

You control very little in life except attitude and effort.
—Bobby Hauck, University of Montana

Lead from the front.
—Chris Fisk, Central Washington University, and Ron Rood, Zillah High School

The goal isn't the end of the road. The goal is the road.
—Frosty Westering, Pacific Lutheran University

Make the big time where you are.
—Frosty Westering, Pacific Lutheran University

Lead by action.
—Larry Donovan, BC Lions

I tell all my coaches you have to have a plan for everything—an objective. You don't just go out day to day and coach. You have a plan you believe in, and you have to be strong enough not to compromise your plan.
—Paul "Bear" Bryant, University of Alabama

Players can learn anything you are smart enough to teach them.
—Tom Ingles, Puyallup High School

You must win at all three levels (frosh, JV, and varsity) to develop a great program.
—Tom Ingles, Puyallup High School

Play with a chip—get after it.
—Brian Burdick, Charles Wright Academy

Nothing but the best; the best is yet to come.
—Mark Venn, Lindbergh High School

Let's keep our weaknesses before us as we grow them.
—Stephanie Dunn, Mt. Paran Christian School

No signs of weakness.
—Pat Ruel, Seattle Seahawks

Change your best.
—P. J. Fleck, University of Minnesota

Follow if needed; lead if necessary.
—Gary Darnell, American Football Coaches Association

A coach's memory needs to be like a scoreboard: at the end of the game, it always gets turned off and reset to zeroes.
—Rick Noren, St. Martin's University

It's not what you say in life that matters; it's what you do.
—Rich Brooks, University of Oregon

Hair on fire—a serious bias for action.
—Jud Keim, Pacific Lutheran University

We set our own standard of excellence.
—Steve Cain, University of Puget Sound

Leaders are never crafty or sneaky.
—Gary Darnell, American Football Coaches Association

If you don't add logs to the fire, the fire goes out.
—Gary Darnell, American Football Coaches Association

If it is going to be, it is up to me.
—Mike Roberts, Franklin Pierce High School

Take great pride in your work.
—R. C. Slocum, Texas A & M University

Things are never as bad as they seem. Things are never as good as they seem. Reality is somewhere in between.
—Jim Christopherson, Concordia University, Minnesota

Coach them up, not down.
—Skip Hall, Boise State University

Encouragement is the fuel that propels us.
—Skip Hall, Boise State University

You're better than that.
—Frosty Westering, Pacific Lutheran University

EMAL—Every man a leader.
—Luke Balash, North Pole High School

As the game (or season) gets longer, we get stronger.
—Kirk Talley, Warner University

Up to now, we have had too many chiefs and not enough Indians.
—Unknown

Get a goal. Then get rid of those things in your life that keep you from attaining that goal.
—Unknown

Contrary to the opinion of many people, leaders are not born. Leaders are made, and they are made by effort and hard work.
—Vince Lombardi, Green Bay Packers

As a coach, having a player with great leadership skills is always worth points in our back pocket before the game even starts.
—Janna Hjelseth, Tri-County High School

QUESTIONS TO AFFECT YOUR LIFE

1) Who do you most admire as a leader? Identify three qualities that person models in leadership.

2) We live in a world of corruption and fallen leaders because of moral failure. Why?

3) What do you believe is a common quality found in successful leaders?

4) One of my favorite sayings on leadership is "Lead, follow, or get out of the way."[25] Which are you doing?

RELATIONSHIPS

- The way in which two or more people or things are connected, or the state of being connected
- The way in which two or more people or groups regard and behave toward each other
- A connection, association, or involvement[26]
- A strong, deep, or close association or acquaintance between two or more people[27]
- The state of being related or interrelated[28]
- Synonyms: connection, relation, association, link, correlation, parallel, alliance, bond, interrelation, interconnection; family ties, kinship, affinity

If we believe the Bible's teaching, we know from the book of Genesis that God was pleased with His creation of the universe. However, He felt that something was missing, so He created Adam. Then, because Adam was alone, God created Eve. To provide for them, He gave them free access to and responsibility for everything except one tree.

God wanted and provided relationship—it was His idea. The Bible also says men and women are created in His image. Like Him, we are made for relationship. Perhaps you have heard the saying "God is love." I have always believed that God's love often comes to us through the people He puts in our path.

Take, for instance, the relationship between mother and child. From the time a baby is born, its most fundamental relationship is with its mother. Unless circumstances separate the two, a baby is nurtured, cared for, and loved by its mother from the very first day of its life. At the same time, the role of the father adds to that relationship. A baby's first smile is likely directed toward the person it knows best, usually the mother or father. Over time, many other relationships get added to a child's life: siblings, grandparents, relatives, and friends. As children grow, their relationships extend to include school, college, career, and a variety of other settings. Each of these relationships—whether for a season or a lifetime—is instrumental in shaping a person's life.

WORDS AND LOVE

This book is about relationships as much as it is about words. The words of other people have a significant effect on our lives. Whether they are spoken or written to us by parents, siblings, teachers, coaches, mentors, and so on, words can either add value to our lives or be hurtful. The more significant the relationship, the more significant the effect of that person's words.

The book of Proverbs in the Bible has much to say about both relationships and words. Here are a few examples: "Wounds from a sincere friend are better than many kisses from an enemy ... The heartfelt counsel of a friend is as sweet as perfume and incense ... As iron sharpens iron, so a friend sharpens a friend" (Proverbs 27:6, 9, 17).

When we allow other people to speak into our lives, we can choose whether to receive or reject what they say to us. Ideally their messages affirm who we are or who we have the potential to become. Sometimes words are corrective; these, too, can be helpful.

One of my core beliefs is that people and teams need encouragement—words of support, acknowledgment, affirmation, and applause for what they are doing well. In my experience, withholding affirmation is a mistake. I have yet to hear anyone complain about receiving too much encouragement!

For instance, I have learned that if I want to bring out the best in my wife, I acknowledge the best in her. Alternatively, I could choose to find fault with little things I notice. But I'm sure you would agree that my marital relationship will last longer and be stronger with a positive-seeking strategy! If I want a smile and warm affection from Ronni, I simply affirm the many things she does for our family and me. For example, recently she encouraged me to update my profile photo on social media, so what did I do? I chose a photo of the two of us. Wow, did that get a positive reaction! Not only is it a better photo of me, but now it includes her as well.

Effective parenting requires consistency—consistent actions and consistent messages. For example, I found that my two boys needed a mix of "Way to go!" and "I think you can do better next time." The more sternly I addressed an issue with them, the more I needed to balance that with catching them in the act of doing something well.

The same principle applies to leading groups of people. I learned early in my coaching career that my team needed positive motivation, both as a group and as individual players. As head coach, it was my job to help the assistant coaches do the same. In coaching, it is reflexive to look for and notice things that need correcting, which is important for improvement and future success. Of equal importance, however, is that whether I was coaching the quarterback on a skill on the practice field or making comments to the entire team at the end of a practice, I had to clearly and consistently communicate the message that I cared, appreciated their effort, and saw improvement, and that the team was making progress. It was my responsibility to convince my team that they could do the impossible, I believed in them, competition was meant to be enjoyed, and there was valor in giving our very best effort as a team. By the end of a practice week before game day, I needed to convey through my words that we were ready to succeed. A practice error that prompted stern correction on Monday or Tuesday would be gently acknowledged by our coaches on Friday. Game day was Saturday, and we wanted our team ready to play and believing they would win!

Whether leading a family, a team, or an entire organization, a leader's role is multifaceted. This may include providing vision, direction, and corrective teaching while charting a course for success.

For me, a small—but highly significant—part of empowering success was simply being intentional about smiling at colleagues in the hallway and taking time to affirm what I saw people doing well.

The person you meet in passing—in a room, at a gas pump, or in a store's checkout line—may need just one thing: encouragement. Being a blessing to another person can sometimes be as simple as making eye contact and listening; at other times, it may mean speaking or writing encouraging words. My wife has consistently said, "Ross, I'm not asking you to fix it. I just want to talk about it." This is her way of expressing her need for my attentive ear. In many cases, love requires time and listening.

PUT IT IN WRITING

I am a big believer in handwritten notes to family members, colleagues, and people whom I feel need acknowledgment. Email is efficient, but not very warm—and certainly not motivational. I find handwritten notes to be far more effective. When I notice something done well, I make a note (mental or written) and later make time to send those responsible a handwritten note of acknowledgment or thanks. As I walked in and out of the classrooms and offices at the school I led for twenty-six years, it was both humbling and encouraging to see those handwritten notes taped to the edges of computer screens, pinned on bulletin boards near colleagues' desks, or otherwise proudly displayed.

I was also known to walk into an executive team meeting with a stack of note cards and envelopes. On those occasions, our team would spend part of our meeting time writing notes of affirmation and encouragement to those we were leading. A shepherd's job is to care for the sheep. Taking five minutes to write a note can infuse a relationship with a lifetime of goodwill.

LOVING WELL = LIVING WELL

Dr. Fulton Buntain served as the senior pastor at Life Center in Tacoma, Washington, for more than forty years. During his ministry, he developed a collection of sayings that he had printed on cards that he called "chin lifters." One of these sayings was "The better you love, the better you live." From the pulpit, Fulton would pause his message to have the congregation repeat this phrase several times. His exhortation was simple: to love well is to live well. Fulton would often include examples of situations in our lives within which we could apply love. According to Fulton, love was always a viable answer.

Fulton advised that in relationships—whether we're beginning, growing, or mending them—"someone has to go first." In challenging relationships, one person needs to be willing to move things to a better place. This may include apologizing for an offense, whether intended or not; expressing empathy and understanding of the other person's perspective; and/or initiating a safe and positive conversation about the issue. Another way of going first is to take action that demonstrates a sincere effort to improve. Sending a card or small gift, doing a task, delivering a meal, or other gestures all communicate a desire to love, serve, and be in relationship.

LOVE. SPEAK LIFE. PRAY.

Bobb Absten, alongside whom I worked for nine years at Life Christian Academy, took it upon himself to create what became our school's four core values. Each one is about relationships:

> Love God.
> Love others.
> Speak life.
> Pray powerful prayers.

First, Bobb called us to know and "Love God" as our primary and most important relationship. Being in right relationship with

God helps us align all aspects of our lives. This also allows us to better relate to the people whom God puts in our path each day.

"Love others" addresses the ways in which we interact with the people in our lives. We may never know the burdens or brokenness other people are carrying on any given day. However, by sincerely loving people the way God loves us, we can provide the hope, encouragement, or care someone may need.

"Speak life" means using positive words that are encouraging and uplifting—not only in face-to-face conversations, but in correspondence, on social media, and even in class assignments. We all have experienced the power of the spoken or written word. Bobb's goal was to create and sustain a culture in which faculty, staff, students, and parents alike would choose to use words to encourage. This, in turn, helped foster an atmosphere that was warm, relational, and caring.

"Pray powerful prayers" was Bobb's way of urging us to pray, not only in the moment, but with consistency and urgency for the needs of others. He also taught us that our prayers are powerful because we serve a powerful God.

In our leadership team meetings, Bobb would often reference one or more of these core values as it applied to a situation we were navigating. Today these four simple phrases continue to be displayed on the school's walls and throughout its communication pieces, as well as included in orientation training for all employees.

CARE FIRST

Ben Newman is a successful performance coach from St. Louis. I first met Ben through my son Tyler, who is a financial adviser with Northwestern Mutual. Ben was a frequent speaker at Northwestern Mutual conferences and training sessions. I had the opportunity to sit in on several of Ben's sessions and invited him to speak at Life Christian Academy's high school commencement in 2015.

According to Ben, "One of the most important things we can do as a coach is to identify the heartbeat of each individual player and what drives him or her. If we only teach process or action, but we don't understand the hard wiring of the individual player, we will never help them reach their full potential. When we affect the heart first, then they're thinking we can then help them drive to their highest levels of performance." I believe Ben's point was that we reach people when we demonstrate to them that we really care.[29]

IT'S ALL ABOUT PEOPLE

For more than three decades, Jerry Korum has been my best friend. We met in 1986, seated at the same table for a men's ministry Bible study on a Friday morning. I was the head football coach at the University of Puget Sound, and Jerry owned one of the Pacific Northwest's largest and most successful car dealerships. What did we have in common? Really not much, beyond the fact that we were both there to study the Bible and learn.

Over the years, however, our friendship grew. We have shared holidays with our respective families, played rounds of golf, shared numerous lunches and coffees, and communicated almost daily via the phone or in person. As our friendship has grown, and we've each grown individually, I have learned a lot from Jerry. I always feel like I'm a better man after I spend time with him. When I'm around him, I see how well he relates to people. As he has told me, the car is important, but the relationship sells. Jerry built relationship by caring for other people, and as a result, he gained customers for life.

Here's one quick story about Jerry's relational touch. One year ago, his grandson Joe was chosen by his peer students to be a member of Life Christian Academy's homecoming royal court. Jerry attended the game, and I invited him to walk the sidelines with me for a while. In the course of thirty minutes, I may have introduced him to twelve people who were down on the field for various reasons: a team doctor, a photographer, school personnel with supervisory duties, and stadium workers. As I watched my friend connect with people, it was obvious that he is a master relationship builder. He listens well and affirms well. Every person in front of him was made to feel important. Why has Jerry been so successful at selling cars? Because of the feelings he creates in people.

Jerry is also detailed and disciplined. He knows why he can be successful as well as the how-to of succeeding. Many have sought his mentorship over the years, which led him to craft what he calls his "A to Z of Success," a tool he shares with anyone who seeks his input. To anyone who has met Jerry, it's no surprise that many of the letters in his "alphabet" stand for words that have to do with relationship, caring, persevering, and following through on opportunity:

A TO Z OF SUCCESS IN LIFE

Attitude is the key to relationships, happiness, and emotional health. Attitude trumps ability. Believe in God, and believe in yourself.

Believe in truth, possibility, and potential, and expect that belief to bring new opportunities to life.

Creativity gives us the ability to see a bigger picture of a more complete and fascinating life, a life of what can be.

Don't do business alone. Gather people around you for greater results. None of us is as smart as all of us. "As iron sharpens iron, so one sharpens another."

Energy and health are by-products of a nourished body and mind.

Fun renews and reenergizes us. The person who laughs, lasts.

Growth is the expression of our being. We are designed to grow. If we are not growing, we are dying.

Humility has an attraction that draws others to us.

Invitation is vital. People are happiest when they have received or given an invitation.

Jesus gives us the tools and principles to live well. Look at what He said and did. Execute on His teachings and win.

Kindness creates confidence and fosters genuine friendships.

Listening shows others that we value them as well as respect them.

Money is nice, necessary, and important. Have a plan for it to ensure financial security throughout your life.

Never, ever give up on your dreams. A dream is like a wonderful plant. It takes off and must be nourished with good thinking, care, vision, and determination.

Open your mind to great possibilities. The mind is powerful. Opening it to dreams and possibilities will ensure its continual expansion.

Preparation creates the road map for life. The level of preparation determines the level of success.

Quit looking where you have been and start looking where you want to be.

Respect yourself and respect others equally. This is the foundation of self-discipline and personal power.

Stickability is the ability to stay with your goal until it produces results.

There is no right way to do the wrong thing.

Understand first, then act.

Victory is there for those who see it clearly enough and want it badly enough.

Work isn't your curse; it's your art.

X marks the spot where you are. Plan for the future but live in the moment.

Your life begins when you give yourself to something greater.

Zest is the passion that energizes our purpose.[30]

PROPEL TO POTENTIAL

Jason Chorak is one of the people I interviewed for this book. You may remember part of his story from the chapter on training. Jason also spoke to me about the key relationships that have helped him reach the next level, including his high school coach, college coaches, and key support personnel. In each case, Jason wanted to please his mentors because he knew they cared for him and believed in him. For example, he told me that Dick Vermeil, head coach of the St. Louis Rams, was demanding of his players, yet they worked hard to meet his expectations because they knew he cared for them. In fact,

Jason said Coach Vermeil was the most passionate man he knew, and that he would cry at team meetings and in locker rooms because of his love for his players and assistant coaches.

Jason also talked about his relationship with Randy Hart, who was Jason's defensive line coach at the University of Washington. Coach Hart taught his players how to play the game, but more importantly, he taught them how to be accountable, work hard, be disciplined, and show appreciation for others. Jason cited timeliness as an example. Coach Hart taught his players that when they were late, it sent the message that the person they were meeting was unimportant and that the person's time wasn't as valuable as their own. Coach Hart expected his players to be on time to honor other people, and he advocated selflessness rather than selfishness. Jason thrived under Coach Hart's leadership, because he knew his coach cared for him and wanted the best for him and his fellow defensive linemen.

In recent years, Jason has successfully engaged in World Ventures, where he is applying the same principles he learned from coaches and influencers in the training and athletic world. The keys for Jason are seeing potential in other people, helping people see a better future, and helping them open their own doors to opportunity. According to Jason, relationships begin and extend through helping people believe in themselves, do the same for others, and take actions to be successful. Relationships are key to network marketing.

RELATIONSHIP MATTERS

Mike Roberts spent a career teaching and coaching football, and he was a valued assistant coach on my staff at the University of Puget Sound. When I reached out to him for input for this book, he shared with me a letter he had received from a former student:

Dear Mr. Roberts,

How are you? I hope well. I am a former student of yours. Who I am really does not matter, but what does matter is the acknowledgment for what you did for me.

After I graduated, I decided not to go to college. I always knew I would go to school, but did not because I didn't know what I wanted to be. The years rolled past, just as you said they would. I found myself with a great girl, a home, and everything I wanted. Or at least I thought I wanted. The girl went away and I found myself trying to be tough and ignore the issues that were building. I began to see myself in a dark corner, fighting off demands that I did not know how to recognize. Fortunately, I kept trying to follow my heart, and it led me back to school. Here I thought all those issues would go away, because I was doing what I was dreaming of doing. They did not. I found a gun to my head, trying to understand problems I was incapable of solving myself. I could not find help with my family, and I only had one person in that corner that was giving me all that I needed. And that was his love. That person was you, Mr. Roberts. I found my way to help because of your teachings. I found my way to help because you cared.

I am about to graduate and go on with this wonderful life. I am doing my best, because that is what I am capable of doing. You are a great man, Mr. Roberts, and I hope someday that I can pass on what I've learned. And I hope they listen, because that could mean the difference between a great life and the one you end up with.

God bless you and your family. Good day.

Sincerely yours,
Former student

Never underestimate the power of relationship and our potential effect on others!

PLAY THE LONG GAME

I have developed a great deal of respect for Mike Colbrese, who has served as executive director of the Washington Interscholastic Activities Association since 1993, a remarkably long tenure among leaders of state associations of schools. At a recent retirement event to honor Mike, I listened as school leaders from around the state affirmed his success and influence as a relational leader. He is perceived as a friend and a voice for all—well known or unknown, urban or rural, east or west. When I met with Mike to get his insight into leadership, he explained that the key for him was one word: *relationships.* He strives to care, listen, ask the right questions, and help create solutions.

When Mike was hired, his board advised him to get out and meet the organization's member schools and their people. The board also suggested that he visit 10 percent of the schools each year, so that he was touching base with all member schools. This meant large schools and small ones, urban and rural locations, covering the full geography of the state. By jumping in his car on a regular basis and going to meet, talk with, and listen to people, Mike became one of them and was welcome in their schools, at district meetings, and at state events. He also broke down any walls that had previously existed between schools, districts, and the WIAA. Mike said the fact that he had sat around the table and talked with people made a significant difference in times of conflict. Although there may have been disagreement, the relationship of caring, listening, and trust remained intact. Trust had been built over time and withstood the tests that arose along the way.

Mike also spoke about the importance of his staff knowing that he cared for them. He made sure his team knew that he had their backs, and that they could trust him to do the right thing in the best interests of all. Mike was also intentional about nurturing his staff's passion for their work and care for each other. Shared passion, he said, helps people get through difficult challenges and keeps an organization moving forward. Mike worked to create a sense of family among his staff.

Mike noted that relationships can be injured by overreacting to emotions. His advice was "Don't take it personal" when attacks or challenges occur, but instead do your best as a leader to disarm the issue, and to listen carefully to a diverse cross section of people to get a full understanding of the perspectives and feelings involved. The more relationships that leaders cultivate, the more effective their leadership.

PUT PEOPLE FIRST

One of the most intriguing conversations I have had in the past year was with George Pilant. George has worked since 1990 in residential real estate sales, and he's currently a partner with my son Brandon in Hjelseth/Pilant Real Estate in the greater Tacoma area. When I shared with George my proposed list of chapter topics and asked him which had been most relevant to his success, he immediately said, "Relationships." Here's a transcript of his comments about the importance of relationships in a sales career.

> Developing trusting and loyal relationships is the key to success. In sales, there are two methods of building a successful business:
>
> 1. The transactional way, where it's all about the numbers—how many calls you make, how many leads you create, how many no's you hear before getting a yes.
> 2. The relational way, where you far exceed the client's expectations with your product or service, and turn the client into a loyal fan who hires you again and again, and refers you and your service to others.

In sales, the transactional way is more expensive, as it requires a greater dependence on advertising dollars and generally comes with lower profit margins. If you are always competing on price and having to advertise to get more clients, it costs you more, in both time and money. And no amount of advertising can overcome a bad experience or bad reputation.

With relational sales, you can build a very successful repeat-and-referral business that will continue to grow if you continually demonstrate through your work that you can be trusted, you know what you are doing, and you will put your client's needs ahead of your own. If you are selling a product, the same applies. Will your company produce a great product that will work as intended, and will you stand behind your product if something should go wrong?

George related an example that illustrates his work and learnings:

One of my best referral sources in real estate is someone who never bought or sold a home with me! I was called in to talk with a couple about the market value of their current home and making a move to a new home. They needed to make a change because they didn't think they could "age in place" in their current home. They had hired an architect to make changes to their home, but when they priced out the architect's expansive and expensive remodel, the costs were more than they could afford. So they thought they would have to sell their home and leave the neighborhood they loved to find a home where they could age in place.

It was clear to me they didn't want to move, but they didn't see a way to change their home that they could afford. I asked, "If there was a way you could make affordable changes to your home that would enable you to stay here and not sell or move, would you be interested?" They said yes. I borrowed a tape measure and within a short time sketched out a first-floor remodel that would allow them to age in place and stay in the home they loved.

Technically, I lost two sales and a chance for considerable profit. But I gained loyal fans who have since referred me to many other people who have bought and sold homes with me, and who, in turn, have referred others to me as well. This is what comes from putting your client's needs first.

When I asked George what he attributed his success to, this was his answer:

Always putting my client's needs before my own and helping them make the best decisions for themselves and their families has enabled me to build a successful business. Keeping my skills sharp and working with a servant's heart has provided me with a continually expanding network of loyal repeat and referring clients—and quite a few friends.

SAYINGS

I love my squad, and I tell them. We have love on our squad, togetherness.
—Tony Mason, University of Arizona

Football on Saturday should be fun for the players. It's not fun practicing, so on Saturday you might as well enjoy it, because you have paid the price all week.
—Joe Paterno, Penn State University

Life is all about relationships, vertical and horizontal. Love God and love one another.
—Chris Softley, Lubbock Christian School

Individually, it's a whole lot different, and you have to learn what makes this or that Sammy run. For one, it's a pat on the back. For another, it's chewing him out. For still another, it's a fatherly talk or something else. You're a fool if you think, like I did as a younger coach, you can treat them all the same.
—Paul "Bear" Bryant, University of Alabama

Chemistry is having coaches enjoy coaching and teammates enjoy playing the game.
—Fred Goldsmith, Rice University

We're a family on the field, so leave all the problems at home.
—Arthur Sanchez, Concrete High School

Popular ain't always right. Right ain't always popular.
—Johnny Tusa, Waco High School

Be loquacious.
—Erik Brown, Eldorado High School

Show me your friends, and I will show you your future.
—Travis Neikamp, Illinois State University

If you don't love parents, get out of coaching.
—Tom Ingles, Puyallup High School

The power of respect is to never disrespect.
—Pat Ruel, Seattle Seahawks

Love is action.
—Brian Jensen, Bellarmine Preparatory School

Players don't care how much you know, until they know how much you care.
—Dick Vermeil, St. Louis Rams

Being tough is sometimes not the most compassionate thing to do.
—Gary Darnell, American Football Coaches Association

Trust your buddy.
—Bill Alexander, Quincy High School

Football is a means to an end. What will you do when you can no longer play?
—Earl Casey Banks, Morgan State University

It's when I stop chewing your ass in practice that you should worry. That's a sign I have given up on you.
—Jim Dew, Valley City State University

Treat a sub like a star, and treat a star like a sub.
—Phil Hayford, Keswick Christian School

He must treat some with the gentleness of a loving mother, and others with the forcefulness of a strong father.
—Richard L. Hardy

The crowd at your funeral will depend on the weather. If it's a nice day, you'll get a nice turnout. If it's cold or the wind is blowing off Lake Michigan, there won't be many people there. So do your job and try to find a certain amount of happiness in it.
—Al Maguire, Marquette University

Great Spirit, grant that I may not criticize my neighbor until I have walked a mile in his moccasins.
—Indian prayer

Appreciate each other's problems. Be compassionate and understanding. When kids feel unity, they become united.
—Tony Mason, University of Arizona

I always told my coaches that as a staff, two things have to happen. One is you have to have fun, and two is that we have to be successful. If either of these is not happening, then get out of the game. All you have is the love of the game, your players, and the coaches.
—Dick Zatkovich, Lincoln High School

The hardest thing to do in life is listen.
—Eddie Jones, Blinn College

The best coaching is less coaching.
—Rahman Sparks, Redan High School

Players win games; coaches lose them.
—Rahman Sparks, Redan High School

You can be rich and live poor, or you can be poor and live rich.
—Gary Darnell, American Football Coaches Association

Don't mistake kindness for weakness.
—Gary Darnell, American Football Coaches Association

At NDSU, we never cared who scored the winning touchdown or who made the play of the game. We only cared about each other. We loved each other.
—Chuck Rodgers, North Dakota State University

We provide young people the opportunity to see how good they can be.
—Pat Simmers, North Dakota State University

I'm so proud of you.
—Dave Collins, Hope Community Church

Coaching is a people business that is results oriented. As coaches, we are coaching others who will make things happen.
—Mike Dunbar, University of California, Berkeley

The value of athletics is found in the lessons learned in practice, competition, and as a team member. Athletics are a vehicle for student-athletes to develop the performance and coping skills that will prepare and see them through the greatest competition of all: life.
—Bob Lucey, Curtis High School

He must get a lot of his satisfaction from the young men who come back and say, "Thank you, Coach." He must be proud of the word "coach," because that makes him special.
—Richard L. Hardy

QUESTIONS TO AFFECT YOUR LIFE

1) How do you think relationships are best built?

2) What do you look for in a relationship with another person—family member, teammate, coach, or colleague?

3) How did God prove He is a God of relationship? What evidence do we have?

4) How do words help or hurt relationships? Have you lived an example of each that you can easily recall?

5) What is one step you could take to begin building more positive relationships?

TEAMWORK

- The combined action of a group, especially when effective and efficient
- Teamwork is the collaborative effort of a team to achieve a common goal or to complete a task in the most effective way. This concept is seen within the greater context of a team, which is a group of interdependent individuals who work together toward a common goal. Basic requirements for effective teamwork include clearly defined roles within the team in order for everyone to have a clear purpose. Teamwork is present in any context where a group of people is working together to achieve a common goal.[31]
- Synonyms: collaboration, working together, joint action, combined effort, mutual support, partnership, coordination, liaison, association, synergy, unity, concurrence, concord, accord, understanding, give and take, compromise

A team is a group of individuals working together to achieve their goal. As defined by Professor Leigh Thompson of the Kellogg School of Management, "A team is a group of people who are interdependent with respect to information, resources, and skills, and who seek to combine their efforts to achieve a common goal."[32, 33]

A team becomes more than just a collection of people when a strong sense of mutual commitment creates synergy, thus generating performance greater than the sum of the performance of its individual members.[34]

TEAMWORK > TALENT

The team is greater than the sum of its parts. In athletics, for example, players realize that coming together to succeed is the means by which championships may be won, even by teams with less talent than some of their opposition. Championship game interviews with members of the winning team after the game often include statements like these:

> The best team won.
> Our team came together.
> We loved one another.
> We sacrificed for the team.
> We wanted it more.
> We believed in one another.

Such statements refer to the uniqueness of a group of people coming together, playing together, and achieving at a high level. The best coaches know how to help their players become a team, and the most talented team doesn't always win.

The sayings at the end of this chapter about teamwork come from a variety of coaches, leaders, and high achievers. Each has developed a philosophy on how to bring a group together to accomplish great things and attain substantial goals.

I was fortunate to be an assistant football coach at North Dakota State University from 1977 to 1985. In several of those seasons, our teams competed for—and sometimes won—conference and national championships. Our 1981 and 1982 teams both finished their respective seasons in the national playoffs among the finest teams in NCAA Division II, and both teams came up just short of taking home the big trophy.

The 1983 team retained a strong nucleus of players from the previous two years and was favored to return to the national playoffs. That season had a different feel, however, with a freshman at starting quarterback and two freshman running backs. It is no small feat to integrate new players into a veteran team, especially when the lineup includes veterans at many positions. Nonetheless, that new collaboration led to a dream season. From the outset, our coaching staff, led by head coach Don Morton, exhorted the group to become "the ultimate team," in which the team was greater than the sum of its parts. The result? NDSU, with freshmen at key positions, won the North Central Conference championship and continued to the postseason playoffs.

The team went on to defeat Central State of Ohio in the Palm Bowl in McAllen, Texas, on December 10 by a score of 41–21. Although Central State had many high-quality athletes, the Bison exerted their will as the best team and established a solid first-half lead, further increasing their lead in the second half. By the end of the game, it was clear this hybrid team had indeed become the ultimate team, achieving a goal the NDSU teams of the two previous years had not, though those earlier teams may well have had more talent.

The team is greater than the sum of its parts.

TEAM FOR ALL SEASONS

My eldest son, Brandon, became a solid golfer between eighth grade and eleventh grade, because his best friend, Taylor Ferris, was a more accomplished player and a great teacher. In their sophomore season, they competed on a local public high school's team because Life Christian Academy did not offer a golf program. Between their sophomore and junior years, they asked Don "Gus" Gustafson, an avid golfer and a coach in other sports, to be their head golf coach. Gus agreed to do so, and the 2002 season concluded with an impressive seventh-in-state placing for the newly formed team.

When the 2002 season ended, Taylor and Brandon kept working. They spent much of the summer, fall, and even winter months together, improving their individual games and playing together. Their goal was to win a state championship in just the second year as a Life Christian Academy team.

The WIAA offers a two-day state tournament schedule. At the

end of day one, the Eagles team was in a solid position but trailed Royal, the previous year's state champions. To win the state title, both Taylor and Brandon knew they needed to overtake the Royal team by shooting lower second-round scores. As the second day of the tournament wore on, it became obvious the state title would be determined on the back nine. Brandon shot the low score for the second round among all players, and Taylor won the low two-day total. The Eagles had won their first state golf championship! All those hours and hours of practice had made them a team and enabled them to play to the level they needed to be state champions!

TEAM LEARNING

When I was a young boy, learning was entirely a function of listening to my teacher and then doing my work, with no help from my classmates. Rarely did our teacher allow us to work together on an assignment. In graduate school in the 1980s, I experienced a bit of group learning when several of us were assigned to work on a project together.

Since then, teamwork has gained increasing traction as an accepted methodology in education theory. In today's classrooms, collaborative learning is a significant presence at all levels of education. One may visit any school and see desks arranged in learning circles or grouped into tables where students interact with one another. Students work individually at times, but a good portion of classroom time is spent using peer observation and discussion to complete assignments and projects. Teachers, who are also learning collaboratively from each other, use a variety of teaching methods to help their students achieve at a high level, as well as develop their social and emotional levels of interaction.

Several years ago, I brought a new leadership development program to Life Christian Academy. It was called Student Leadership Institute (SLI), and its focus was the intentional cultivation of leadership skills among high school students. For the first three years, we brought in speakers, did group-reads of leadership-focused books, and held discussions of the content. The students worked in discussion groups a good share of the time. The fourth year, however, I wanted to increase students' engagement and accountability for their learning.

I decided to introduce the "Harkness method," named for Edward Harkness, an alumnus and philanthropist of St. Paul's School. Harkness had given Phillips Exeter Academy a gift that was used to develop a new method of teaching and learning. According to the Harkness method, students sit around an oval table that allows all of them to see and hear one another. Instead of a teacher standing at the front of the room and students focusing on the teacher, the interaction involves the teacher guiding the discussion while the students are responsible for engaging in listening or adding to the discussion.

SLI adopted this method with the intent of teaching future leaders that they were responsible for engaging as active participants. Without question, the new structure was effective. I distributed case studies to all SLI students before each session and communicated the expectation that they read and be prepared to participate in discussing the material. As each session led to the next, the students learned to voice their insights, objections, or support, and they became increasingly adept and confident in doing so. They also learned to follow the conversation and listen to the point of understanding their peers' viewpoints.

Every day, in business, government, and nonprofit organizations around the world, leaders come to meetings prepared to discuss key strategic items. Those leaders also expect their team members to be prepared for input, discussion, and decision making as a team. The Harkness method helped prepare Life Christian Academy's high school students for future meetings of this type in their chosen careers. As I look back on the first five years of SLI at LCA, I am fondest of the use of the Harkness method for engaging future leaders.

Some years ago, I attended a conference at Gordon College in suburban Boston. One day the conference met at the Harvard

Graduate School of Business. Beyond the visit to the buildings and lecture halls, the most intriguing part of the day for me was the afternoon spent at the Harvard Innovation Lab, a creative learning environment where students work in teams to advance their innovative project or entrepreneurial focus. The I-lab provides all the physical and intellectual resources current Harvard students need to develop and grow, including one-on-one advising, office hours with industry experts, workshops, an incubator program, and a competition. Open coworking space is available for any Harvard student who wants to grow as an innovator.

The Venture Incubation Program (VIP) is the cornerstone program of the Innovation Lab. It creates a pathway for students to become innovators once their ideas are ready to become ventures. The VIP is a collection of teams, each of which focuses on an innovative venture that shows potential to find a market for a new product launch. In many cases, a venture may be launched with private funding or be bought by an existing business as a part of its acquisition strategy.

The Harvard Innovation Lab and its Venture Incubation Program are noteworthy examples of learning in teams. As students spend a year working together, they become immersed in their innovative venture by effectively working as a team. Team works at Harvard.

TEAM BUILDING

Over the past thirty years, ropes courses have become increasingly popular as resources for team building. Organizations, groups, departments, and teams have used these interactive, challenging courses to help team members better understand their reliance on one another. The ropes are positioned to require complicated movements and balance-related activities that can successfully be completed only by all team members working together. Instead of the boss or leader simply demanding teamwork, the ropes course effectively teaches team members that to accomplish the grid of activities, they must partner with and depend on each other.

I have participated in ropes courses as both a team member and a team leader. As an employee participant, I learned more about my coworkers through communication, strategic thinking, timing of decision making, step-by-step progression, and continued reliance on all members of my group. The most effective group became the one that learned together. This hands-on collaborative learning about teamwork helped strengthen relationships among our employees.

As a leader who took teams through a course, I wanted to increase our team chemistry and potential for success. I knew the ropes course would provide firsthand experience in building relationships as well as acceptance of each other, group goal achievement, and shared realization that they had accomplished the course most successfully because they had done so as a team.

In every instance, during the weeks and months after the experience, we all frequently recalled instances of teamwork in navigating the ropes course. These reminders became long-standing positive affirmations that the team had done it together.

CRITICAL CARE

One of the more complex illustrations of teamwork can be found in the medical profession. Teamwork is essential in the health care world, which is all about patient care. Doctors and attending nurses play key roles, but without the work of X-ray and lab technicians, front desk receptionists, insurance support professionals, physical therapists, and various other specialists, the work of doctors and nurses would be far more difficult. All of these people factor into the teamwork needed to successfully care for each patient.

Whether in a clinic or hospital setting, the patient is there to receive care from well-educated medical professionals. The testing, data collection, and preparation for doctor interpretation are all part of the nurse's role. The patient's relevant data, which may include anything from heart rate and temperature to lab or scan results, is transferred through charts and electronic data to the doctor for interpretation and evaluation before interaction with the patient. This exchange of information, together with the doctor's instructions, results in steps of care that the nursing team administers until the doctor's next interaction with the patient. All of this takes place between two key professionals and the patient. A doctor and a nurse, through fine-tuned teamwork in data collection, communication, interpretation, analysis, and further next steps or directions, guide the patient back to health. This is optimum patient care.

In the case of hospital patient care, teamwork includes more people, since shift changes take place every eight hours or so to provide continuous care. Consequently, over a twenty-four-hour period, at least three nurses must coordinate to provide information about each patient to the doctors responsible during a particular shift. Teamwork at every junction of information flow among these professionals is critical in order for the patient to receive continuous optimum care for the length of his or her treatment. Once again, team works!

ROLES MATTER

In many team sports, the various team members play distinct roles. In baseball, for example, the catcher's responsibility to the team is entirely different from the pitcher's. Outfielders' assignments and skill sets are different from those of infielders'. First basemen's roles are different from those of third basemen. In football, offensive and defensive linemen have entirely different roles, yet they play on the same team. The placekicker's skills are different from those of the punter, yet both are key players in special teams play. Although players' respective positions may be quite different, the sport requires that they all play their roles with excellence to help the team work. Teams with great players in key positions have opportunities to be very good.

Well-run organizations use a similar approach when defining the specific roles employees play. These organizations function as a team and build their reputations based upon how well they work together.

Organizations typically have an "org chart" that clearly defines the relationships of employees to one another. The org chart also defines, to a great degree, the scope of responsibility each employee holds, as well as the connections and communication flow between various areas of the organization. For example, if the company sells a product, the org chart would likely call for the salespeople to communicate with the sales manager before communicating with the CEO or owner of the company. This provides the best opportunity for information flow as well as alignment of team departments and members with the mission of the organization.

The organization chart also defines supervisory roles for people who are responsible for groups of team members or employees. The supervisor or leader of a department needs to ensure that all of his or her team members understand their roles—as individuals within their department, as a department within the organization, and relative to the roles of other groups or departments. This can be accomplished by providing clear job descriptions that specifically define the roles and responsibilities of each employee. Equipped with this information, employees are empowered to work effectively and efficiently within their teams and the organization as a whole.

Businesses and nonprofits want to perform at an optimum level to best serve their customers or clients. This objective is often supported not only through an effective org chart and clear job descriptions, but also through constructive employee evaluations or performance reviews. Based on job descriptions, performance reviews are periodic one-on-one conversations between supervisors and their employees about how well the employees are completing their responsibilities. The dialogue might include noting what is being done successfully or exceptionally well, discussing areas where improvement may be needed, and talking about resources that employees think would help them perform their roles more effectively. These periodic check-ins help group leaders stay connected to each member of their team and provide a framework for continuously strengthening each team member's contribution as well as the team overall. A department that does well with its employee evaluations becomes a solid team that communicates well, understands its function, and knows how it is contributing to the health of the larger organization.

Another exciting team dynamic involves getting the right players on the team and in the right positions. Just as important as choosing good people is knowing the best fit for each member within the team. For example, a person with an introverted personality may play a role that is entirely different from that of a highly social individual. Both may be valuable employees, but they each need to be in a position that fits their particular skills and style. Having the "best people in the best seats on the bus" has become a common way of expressing this process of choosing good people and guiding them into the proper roles.

The best teams comprise players who clearly understand their roles, love being together, and enthusiastically advance the mission of the organization each day. The best teams succeed!

BETTER TOGETHER

I conclude this chapter with one of my favorite encounters with effective teamwork in action. It took place with one of the last teams I coached in my career.

Life Christian Academy's 2007 football team returned a solid offensive line and a solid defensive front from the 2006 team that had finished third in the state. However, the 2007 team had lost most of the "skill" players at quarterback, running back, and receiver, as well as the defensive secondary. Going into the season, this LCA squad was not favored to return to the state playoffs.

However, no one thought to tell that group of young players that they would not do as well as the team that had preceded them. Instead, they came together as a team and won game after game—not with a great offense, but instead with solid defense, ball-control offense, and a solid kicking game. That team won tough playoff games in the round of sixteen, then in the round of eight, finally losing in the semifinals in the Tacoma Dome to a better DeSalles team.

I will never forget the 2006 and 2007 teams, but for different reasons. The 2007 team worked together to offset some known weaknesses by capitalizing on their strengths, and as a result, they won games instead of allowing themselves to lose. As the season extended into the playoffs, it was obvious to everyone that this group of young men had become a cohesive unit, and the missing skill players were not a factor. Like the 2006 team before them, the 2007 Eagles also finished third in state, and they did so as a team!

SAYINGS

It is amazing what can be accomplished when no one cares who gets the credit.
—Harry Truman, president, United States of America, and Chuck Rodgers, North Dakota State University

T.E.A.M. Together Everyone Achieves More
—R. C. Slocum, Texas A & M University

There is no "I" in team.
—Bob Lucey, Curtis High School

ATF—Always Team First
—Kent Nevin, Fife High School

It takes us all to make us one heart.
—George Crace, Pacific Lutheran University

No superstars, only teammates.
—Kent Nevin, Fife High School

Successful teams are a family of one.
—Ken Rucker, University of Texas

Better players don't win; better teams win.
—Jeff Monken, U.S. Army

You guys are in charge of the gas pedal. I take care of the brake.
—Todd Bridge, Elma High School

You can do anything if enough people care.
—Gary Darnell, American Football Coaches Association

The most unselfish teammates accept personal responsibility for their failures on the field.
—Rick Noren, St. Martins University

Team, team, team, it's all about us.
—Miles Hookstead, University of Dubuque

We come together like a fist, fists in the middle together.
—Todd Bridge, Elma High School

We are better when we work together.
—Dave Miller, Lakes High School

There are no great coaches without great players.
—Bill Kiefer, Wahpeton High School

On a team, more so than any other organization, race and religion have absolutely no bearing on acceptance. Performance is the only thing that marks a man.
—Ara Parseghian, University of Notre Dame

A team is where a boy can prove his courage on his own. A gang is where a coward goes to hide.
—Mickey Mantle, New York Yankees

Do your own job.
—Larry Donovan, BC Lions

Everything matters.
—Travis Niekamp, Illinois State University

There is no royalty in football.
—Jerry Rosburg, Baltimore Ravens

Hard work works.
—Brian Jensen, Bellarmine Preparatory School

Preach the importance of team and sacrifice for your brothers. We all need to be servant warriors for the brotherhood.
—Randy Davis, Orting High School

Special teams, defense, and then offense.
—Bill Manlove, Widener University

You don't play for the name on the back of your jersey. You play for the name on the front of the jersey and the people in the school it represents.
—Steve Buuck, Faith Lutheran Middle School and High School

I tell our players that they are going to be the best group in the conference, and then I give them the goals for the day's practice on how they will become the best. When I forget to tell them that they will be the best, they remind me to confirm it to them again. They want to hear it and believe it.
—George Papageorgiou, Benedictine College

Let's all exhibit an attitude of gratitude and be yapping or clapping.
—Chris Softley, Lubbock Christian High School

The best offense is the best offense, because the best offense always wins the time of possession, doesn't turn the ball over, and keeps its own defense off the field. When the other team doesn't have the ball, they can't score, but we can.
—Jon Kellett, Oak Harbor High School

Teams will come to try to beat us, but we just want to be us.
—Bobby Miller, Life Christian Academy

None of us is as strong as all of us together.
—Jud Keim, Pacific Lutheran University

No player is more important than the squad, no squad more important than the team, and no team more important than the program.
—Todd Bridge, Elma High School

Don't allow your lockers to sit there for the whole year with the same guy going to the same spot. This is how cliques form. It's up to the leader to watch these things and to take care of them.
—Al McGuire, Marquette University

That word selflessness as opposed to selfishness is what I try to teach.
—Vince Lombardi, Green Bay Packers

Each individual must work and prepare for the opportunity when his team can capitalize on his particular strengths, and he must do everything within his power to help his teammates do likewise. There can be no envy or jealousy, but rather a sincere and eager desire to have the team do well.
—John Wooden, University of California, Los Angeles

Little eyes are upon you. Represent our TEAM on and off the court/field with class.
—Janna Hjelseth, Tri-County High School

QUESTIONS TO AFFECT YOUR LIFE

1) Think of the best example of teamwork you have been part of or witnessed. What stands out about your example? Why is it important to you?

2) In what area of your life do you feel teamwork is lacking?

3) Why do you believe families, organizations, and athletic teams fail to come together into cohesive units?

4) Read 1 Corinthians 12:14–23 and summarize these verses as an illustration of teamwork.

SUCCESS

- The accomplishment of an aim or purpose
- The correct or desired result of an attempt[35]
- Satisfactory completion of something[36]
- The attainment of fame, wealth, or social status
- A person or thing that achieves desired aims or attains fame, wealth, etc.
- Achievement of an action within a specified period of time or within a specified parameter. Success can also mean completing an objective or reaching a goal. Success can be expanded to encompass an entire project or be restricted to a single component of a project or task. It can be achieved within the workplace or in an individual's personal life.[37]
- Synonyms: victory, triumph, favorable outcome, positive result; prosperity, affluence, wealth, riches, comfort, fortune; bestseller, sellout, coup, master stroke, winner, sensation; star, superstar, celebrity, somebody, VIP, luminary, leading light

In October 1936, author and speaker Dale Carnegie released what would become a perennial bestselling book, *How to Win Friends and Influence People*. An anniversary edition published in 1998 bears this subtitle on its cover: *The Only Book You Need to Lead You to Success*. More than eighty years after its first printing, Carnegie's book remains a top seller, can be found on the shelves of bookstores and bookcases across America, and has been translated into almost every known written language.

Why did Carnegie write this book, and why has it been so widely read? He answers the question in its Introduction:

> I have ... been conducting educational courses for business and professional men and women in New York. At first, I conducted courses in public speaking only—courses designed to train adults, by actual experience, to think on their feet and express their ideas with more clarity, more effectiveness and more poise, both in business interviews and before groups.
>
> But gradually, as the seasons passed, I realized that as sorely as these adults needed training in effective speaking, they needed still more training in the fine art of getting along with people in everyday business and social contacts.
>
> The University of Chicago and the United Y.M.C.A. Schools conducted a survey to determine what adults want to study ... That survey revealed that health is the prime interest of adults—and that their second interest is people; how to understand and get along with people; how to make people like you; and how to win others to your way of thinking.
>
> So the committee conducting this survey resolved to conduct such a course ... They searched diligently for a practical textbook on the subject and found—not one ... Since no such book existed, I have tried to write one for use in my own courses. And here it is. I hope you like it.[38]

This is why Carnegie chose to write his book—to provide a guide to lead people to success. Millions of copies later, people continue to apply its principles and achieve the intended results. Carnegie's principles still work, and always will!

SUCCESS IS WHAT YOU MAKE IT

My writing on success in this chapter is about much more than a score on a scoreboard, a dollar amount on a paycheck or in a bank account, a ranking among competitors, or a number of followers or subscribers. All of these are common indicators of success, because we get excited about perceived winners. However, awards and acquisitions are not the only ways to define or measure success.

As you can see at the beginning of this chapter, the definition of success is quite broad and diverse, not limited to a few words or a single outcome. Instead, it may include multiple outcomes based upon a person's circumstances or pursuits. Success may be represented by a trophy, an increased financial portfolio, or a possession. Or it may take the form of improving your health or fitness, replacing a bad habit with a good one, being a steadfast friend, building a strong marriage, preparing a child for adulthood, or keeping a commitment. Looking through a wider lens helps us expand our perception of success, the ways we move toward achieving it, and the virtually unlimited potential for success in all areas of life.

In my opinion, our pursuit of success must be guided by what we consider successful. If we define success by achievement, then our goals must be aligned with the steps necessary to achieve them. Along the way to achieving the goal, we'll see some indicators of progress, which makes both the pursuit and its ultimate outcome satisfying and worthwhile.

Social media and other applications have tapped into this principle with something called a *streak*. Essentially an electronic version of a counter, a streak counts the number of consecutive days you use the app in a certain way. If you miss a day, you must start a new streak from day one. The concept works because it feeds our sense of success. When used, for instance, with a language-learning app or workout program app, it can provide just enough motivation to make the difference between doing the work that day or skipping it—and maybe skipping the next day, and the next. That little counter number can be an ongoing reflection of success, one day at a time. Alcoholics Anonymous does something similar with the chips it awards for one day of sobriety, one month, three months, and so on. And of course, we can do the same thing with a tool as simple as tick marks in a journal or on a sticky note on our mirror. My point is that most big successes are the result of a whole lot of smaller successes, one day or effort at a time, each of which is critical to the journey and worthy of recognition in itself.

What is your definition of success? What are you searching for to be successful? How will you become successful? What will it require from you, and at what cost to you or others? How will you feel upon realizing the goal that represents success for you? I believe we must answer these questions in order to create a path that will become our journey toward success as we define it.

"Thinking," a poem by Walter D. Wintle, paints a picture of success by illustrating the many ways in which our mindsets, beliefs, and attitudes determine our efforts and outcomes, both positive and negative:

> If you think you are beaten, you are;
> If you think you dare not, you won't;
> If you like to win, but don't think you can,
> It's almost a cinch you won't.
>
> If you think you'll lose, you're lost,
> For out in the world you'll find
> Success begins with a fellow's will.
> It's all in a state of mind.
>
> For many a game is lost
> Ere even a play is run,
> And many a coward fails
> Ere even his work is begun.
>
> Think big and your deeds will grow;
> Think small and you'll fall behind;
> Think that you can and you will;
> It's all in a state of mind.

If you think you are out-classed, you are;
You've got to think high to rise;
You've got to be sure of yourself before
You can ever win a prize.

Life's battles don't always go
To the stronger or faster man,
But sooner or later, the man who wins
Is the fellow who thinks he can.[39]

Although success may be the outcome, it can also be the feelings associated with the achievement along the way to the goal. When we feel successful, we are.

JOURNEY, DESTINATION, OR BOTH?

Forrest "Frosty" Westering, who is quoted several times in this book, was one of America's finest college football coaches. He spent most of his coaching career at Pacific Lutheran University in Tacoma, Washington, and wrote several books, including *Make the Big Time Where You Are*. Coach Westering's approach to teaching and coaching was to help his players and everyone else associated with Lute football understand that success was much more than numbers on the scoreboard.

Although his teams were quite successful, Coach Westering was always about the journey. He wanted his players and coaches to realize that the game's outcome was merely one of multiple areas of focus. He was intentional about teaching the values of love, relationship, teamwork, unity, sportsmanship, and fun. Ultimately each of these areas of focus had a much greater effect than game wins and losses in the lives of Coach Westering's players and those who knew him. His teams always played with high levels of energy, enthusiasm, and competitiveness, but they all knew the journey was more important than the score.

Success in today's American culture has become increasingly

visible, in part because of a significant and continued rise in media coverage and accessibility. Correspondingly, we seem to have elevated our regard for success based on the fact that it is continually paraded before us. I want to suggest that this is not the best measurement of success.

Every success begs the question, "What's next?" In fact, many interviewers pose this question to people who have accomplished a significant feat. When the scoreboard is turned off or the performance is complete, what is the result in the lives of those associated with the outcome? Is it the win or award that makes the difference, or was it the journey to the win that was most important?

Arguably the finest player in the history of golf, Tiger Woods recently won his fifteenth major at the 2019 Masters Tournament. I found it interesting that after this significant win, Tiger repeatedly said that his relationships with those closest to him were what made the win significant. Pictures on the eighteenth green after the last putt dropped showed his mother, his children, and other PGA players all celebrating the win. The moment was so much larger than the win itself because all of those people had been a part of the journey. It was evident to me that although this win was important to Tiger, he was really celebrating the journey he had taken to reach it. This accomplishment was the result of a comeback that many people doubted would ever happen. Millions saw the putt drop on the eighteenth hole, but those same people were oblivious to the work, determination, setbacks, challenges, and support it took for that moment to take place.

I particularly remember watching an interview with Nota Begay, Tiger's longtime friend and teammate at Stanford University. When asked whether he had ever doubted that Tiger would make a comeback, Begay said, "Yes, when I visited Tiger at his home shortly after one of his back surgeries." Nota described leaving Tiger after a daylong visit and realizing that his friend needed help to get out of a chair or the seat of a car, and that Tiger could not drive. It seems almost unimaginable that someone in that condition would ever swing a golf club again, let alone win the Masters!

The fans and followers don't see the daily commitment to getting better, overcoming obstacles, and marking progress toward the opportunity to compete in a pinnacle moment. For Tiger, and for every other player who has ever won that event, the journey to win the Masters was much longer and tougher than the tournament itself or the moment the winner becomes apparent. The journey, visible to a relative few, was vastly different from the outcome seen by millions around the world.

ONE DAY AT A TIME

As the head of an organization, a coach, and a participant in the board room, I have been blessed to watch many people journey through their challenges and opportunities. Some endeavors have had happy endings, whereas others haven't been so joyful. Along the way, we need to be careful not to view it all through a simple "win or lose" lens.

One life journey I've had the opportunity to witness firsthand is that of Pat Lynn, a former teacher at Life Christian Academy. Pat's story is one of significant, even exceptional, success, but without public fanfare, cameras, or a scoreboard. Pat taught at LCA for several years and accompanied a number of the school's senior classes on their pregraduation mission trips to Ensenada, Mexico. On one of those trips, Pat asked me how he could get more involved in missions. I introduced Pat to Lourdes Kleid, a youth pastor from New York who led other trips, and she invited Pat to accompany her team on a future trip.

School dismissed for the summer of 2009, and I did not see or hear from Pat much beyond early June. On July 4, as my wife and I walked into a friend's home for a gathering with friends, I noticed I had missed a call and had a message from Lourdes Kleid. My first thought was *Why am I getting a call from Lourdes on the Fourth of July?* In her voicemail message, Lourdes explained that on their mission trip that day, Pat had been involved in a devastating accident.

Their group had been on a hike in the Dominican Republic, and Pat had decided to dive into a river from a bluff, not realizing that the water was quite shallow. He had hit the bottom of the river bed headfirst, which broke his back and completely paralyzed him from the neck down. Because of Pat's significant height and stature, it had been difficult for the responders and team to get him out of the water. This tragic accident led to multiple lengthy hospital stays for Pat, flat on his back with no ability to move his own body. He spent time in hospitals in the Dominican Republic and Miami before being transferred, still paralyzed, to the University of Washington hospital in Seattle in the late summer.

The first time I made the hour-long drive from Tacoma to Seattle to visit Pat, I was uncertain what I would find. My former faculty member was no longer the happy, energetic person I was used to seeing in his classroom. Instead, upon walking into the hospital room, I encountered a Pat who was wide awake and responsive, but the only part of his body that he could move, just slightly, was his right hand. As we talked, I realized the severity of the diving accident. My friend Pat might never move again, and short of a miracle, he wouldn't be returning to teach at Life Christian Academy. Our prayer that day was that we would depend on God and the medical world to bring a positive outcome for Pat, and that we were willing to wait on God's provision of healing.

The next several months of hospitalization and rehabilitation therapy produced some progress, but Pat remained mostly paralyzed. At times the doctors were encouraged, though they were continually cognizant of the damage to Pat's spinal cord that had resulted in his inability to move his arms, hands, and legs. Pat maintained a positive attitude and let his faith in God be his guide. Many in the hospital commented about his resolve and positive demeanor in his approach to the journey ahead. Pat's faith was significant!

Why does Pat Lynn's story appear in this chapter on success? Because in the paragraphs ahead, you will see that his journey does not reflect the typical win-or-lose definition of success. Pat's story, as it continued to unfold, is a testimony to a long journey, inspired by faith, that led to a miraculous outcome for him and his family.

I remember driving to Seattle many times to visit Pat, praying by his bedside, encouraging him, and feeling concerned at times about his lack of progress. I also remember the drives back home, when I had time to think and talk with God about Pat's future. Would he remain motionless in a bed for the rest of his life? Would he experience a breakthrough in his healing and rehabilitation? Would he return to his classroom? Only God and Pat would be able to answer those questions. Success was not going to be immediate; this was going to be a long journey.

Pat's drive, determination, and positive perspective were refreshing to other people. Months later, as he continued to make progress in neurological recovery and muscle development, Pat was able to move his fingers, hands, and toes, but leg movement was slow to return.

Four months after the accident, Pat's doctors decided to release him from the University of Washington hospital; they had done all they could do to help him recover. Although he was happy to leave the hospital, Pat now had to depend on other people to help him with everything from eating to brushing his teeth and bathing himself. I remember Pat sitting in a wheelchair that allowed him to roll himself around. That piece of equipment gave my friend his only independence for months.

One of the truths about success is that it is rarely accomplished alone, and Pat's story is no exception. Family, friends, and others responded with prayers, willingness to help, and generosity to assist Pat in his next phase of adaption and recovery. A room was made available for him at Life Manor, a senior residence and assisted living facility that shares a campus with Life Christian Academy and Life Center. This allowed Pat to be back on campus, in a familiar and positive environment where he could engage with people and life as he had experienced it before his accident. Even today, I clearly remember seeing Pat move about the campus with the assistance of numerous family members and friends.

In our conversations and prayers, Pat would speak of his "someday" dreams, which included being independent, walking again, and doing the things he had enjoyed doing before July 4, 2009. As Pat adapted to his new life in a rolling chair, I got the idea that it was time to get him active in his previous ministry, which had been teaching youth. I asked Pat if he wanted to return to his classroom, even on a part-time basis, and he agreed to do so. Becoming engaged in the life of our school again was good for Pat, because his focus now included students and his faculty colleagues. One of those colleagues was Jennifer Kent, a science teacher we had hired while Pat was in recovery. Pat admitted to me later that Miss Kent had caught his eye!

I remember a conversation in Pat's classroom one morning, during which he spoke of his goal to someday walk across the sanctuary platform at a middle school chapel. We prayed over that dream! As Pat regained strength, he was able to raise himself—with help—out of his wheelchair and stand with the support of two aluminum crutches. From there, he began to shuffle his feet to make progress with the help of the crutches. His first attempts didn't last long, but he kept trying, and each time lasted a bit longer, fueled by his unwavering desire to walk again on his own. Pat progressed to the point where he was ready to make his walk across the stage in front of his students. He did so to rousing applause from our students and staff. What a defining moment in his determination to recover and reach his goal of successfully walking again!

Pat went on to date Jennifer Kent, to whom he is now married. They have two daughters and are building a new home in Sequim, Washington. Throughout the clearing of the land, the construction, and the entire process, Pat has been an on-site, hands-on contractor/owner. He is also employed as a youth pastor. Life is good for Pat Lynn.

Pat is a significant success story in my life. His journey includes no record-setting score, ranking, or award—just his steady, determined, one-day-at-a-time, faith-propelled drive toward the life he envisioned. Well done, my friend!

STEPPING-STONES AND STUMBLING BLOCKS

In my role as head of school, I observed the efforts of countless parents raising their children in a society that, although obsessed with pursuing success, lacks a defined path for facilitating it for today's children and youth. The term *helicopter parents* describes a parenting style in which parents "hover over" their children's experiences and problems. These parents want to constantly oversee their children's lives and avoid allowing them to fail. Unfortunately, this level of involvement by parents ultimately limits the children's development of self-esteem and confidence. Although these parents' intent is well meaning, research and life experience tell us that young people need opportunities to make individual choices and experience the corresponding outcomes in order to develop decision-making and problem-solving skills, as well as self-esteem and confidence.

Effective parenting recognizes appropriate opportunities to allow a child to fail, because failure is one of life's most valuable learning experiences. Most significant achievements, from a toddler learning to walk and run, to the Wright brothers successfully flying a plane or Steve Jobs and Apple launching the iPhone, come only after failed attempts. One of the keys to success is to "keep on keeping on." With failure, we learn and try again. Parents need to let their children fail so that they'll learn how to overcome failure.

Tom Pierson, president and CEO of the Tacoma–Pierce County Chamber of Commerce, spoke with me about successfully serving clients and advancing an organization. He asked, "One hundred years from now, who will be remembered for the impact they made?" This question was his way of highlighting the importance of being intentional in our pursuit of positively influencing other people. Tom's keys to success consists of six elements:

1. Use your diverse background as your strength.
2. Relate to others.
3. Listening matters, so listen well.
4. Be a truth teller, which will define your future in terms of success.
5. Walk the talk, because people value knowing they can depend on you to be who and what you say you are.
6. Trust and be trustworthy; repeat success comes because trust is built.

Tom went on to talk about casting vision and engaging people to join him in moving the vision forward. He explained that talking directly with people is the best possible mode of communication. Sometimes this means having multiple conversations with multiple individuals and groups, until a common awareness is established for all stakeholders. It also may include having tough conversations around unpleasant truths. Does this process take a lot of time and involve some discomfort? Yes, but it also accomplishes the objective by building a stronger foundation for the future.

Finally, Tom defines success as what you see when you look in the mirror. Have you been true to yourself and to others? The person in the mirror can best provide that answer.

You may recall comments in an earlier chapter from Josh Dunn, owner of *425* and *South Sound* magazines. In my conversation with Josh, he shared his principles for creating success within a business and passion for positively influencing the community:

1. Surround yourself with great minds; fill in the voids of your own weaknesses.
2. Provide excellence at all costs; never shortchange the product.
3. Adopt an attitude of servanthood; serve your community.
4. With your staff, elevate the talent around the leader to elevate the team.
5. Get the wise counsel of a good attorney, CPA, and banker.

Each of these recommendations has been lived out by Josh and his team. I can attest to his company's prolific presence in our community and in the neighboring 425 area code as well. His time and efforts reflect not only his vision, but also his values of service and teamwork.

We all can be successful, but the success may be different from what the world recognizes. Most people's success is not determined by a scoreboard, a financial statement, a promotion, or an award. Life is what happens while we are living, and living to be our best self is success each day!

SAYINGS

Three rules to follow if you want to win:

1. *Surround yourself with people who can't live without football.*
2. *Be able to recognize winners—they come in all forms and shapes.*
3. *Have a plan for everything.*
—Paul "Bear" Bryant

Live with a will to win, and give the effort to endure.
—Randy Hart, Stanford University

Fundamentals, discipline, hard work, selflessness, control—these are the visible elements of the Wooden system. But it also includes picking up the soap from the shower, stacking towels, personal grooming, training table diet, and a concept for character building called the pyramid of success.
—John Wooden, University of California, Los Angeles

Only four reasons for failure:
1. *Weren't told*
2. *Not smart enough*
3. *Don't care*
4. *Under negative influence*
—Randy Hart, Stanford University

The wins on the scoreboard keep your job, but the real wins are the hearts of the students you are coaching and leading. They who become winners in life are the real wins.
—Gerry Faust, University of Notre Dame

No question we're the ones who spoil the athlete. We paint a rosy picture: he can play as a sophomore, we're champs. Bunch of malarkey. He'll play as a sophomore if he's good enough. He'll be on a championship team if he sacrifices enough.
—Darrell Royal, University of Texas

The team with the fewest mistakes will win.
—Fred Goldsmith, Rice University, and Nick Kotys, Coral Gables High School

Missed alignments and missed assignments will beat you more than lack of ability.
—Fred Goldsmith, Rice University, and Al Groh, Wake Forest University

Some dogs just won't hunt.
—Jovan Haye, Vanderbilt University

Your success is not just about changing your habits, but also about changing the way you think.
—Ben Newman, Newman Coaching

Winners win.
—Eric Cohu, Little Rock Christian Academy

Full speed is game speed.
—Greg Polnasek, Albion College

Play hard, play smart.
—Oval Jaynes, Wake Forest University

Some guys play with their heads. That's okay. You've got to be smart to be number one in any business. But more important, you've got to play with your heart—with every fiber of your body. If you're lucky enough to find a guy with a lot of head and a lot of heart, he's never going to come off the field second.
—Vince Lombardi, Green Bay Packers

Win the physical battles early.
—Oval Jaynes, Wake Forest University

The biggest threat to success is complacency.
—Jeff Monken, U.S. Army

Win with a positive mental attitude.
—Larry Kindbom, Washington University

Trust the process and love the grind.
—David Calloway, Central Methodist University

Earn victory.
—Larry Prather, Reinhardt University

We will never learn to lose. We will practice to win. We will think like winners. We will act like winners. We will dress like winners. Someday we will eventually win.
—Johnny Majors, University of Tennessee

Championship behaviors all day long.
—Bubba Schweigert, University of North Dakota

Leave this place better than we found it.
—Bill Beattie, Tumwater High School

A football season: a period of time that becomes one big game. Any game can become a season, any minute can produce a game-winning play, and any play can make a winning season.
—George Allen, Washington Redskins

Run to the fight.
—Brian Flattum, Cascade Christian School

The best will be first, but first be your best.
—George Crace, Pacific Lutheran University

Strive for excellence.
—Carey Bogue, Life Christian Academy

Be 1–0 every day in every way.
—Mike Durnin, University of Dubuque

Excuses are justifications for losers.
—Vernon Fox, Faith Lutheran High School

Regardless of what you put into it, every game boils down to doing the things you do best, and doing them over and over again.
—Vince Lombardi, Green Bay Packers

You remember a mistake in direct proportion to how much you suffer when you make the mistake.
—Rich Brooks, University of Oregon

Championships are won by uncommon people because common people are basically lazy.
—Dick Zatkovich, Lincoln High School

It's tough to beat relentless.
—Jud Keim, Pacific Lutheran University

Throw away the word lose. We will either get beat by a better team or we'll beat ourselves, but we will never be losers.
—K. C. Johnson, Adna High School

Work hard every day, improve every day, be unselfish, and be the best.
—Scott Smith, Legacy Christian Academy

Winners never quit. Quitters never win.
—Robert Hunt, Wilson High School, and Vince Lombardi, Green Bay Packers

Success only comes before work in the dictionary. In life, you have to work real hard to have success.
—Mike Roberts, Franklin Pierce High School

Six seconds to success. A football play lasts approximately six seconds, so we practice in six-second bursts.
—Mike Roberts, Franklin Pierce High School

If it is going to be, it is up to me.
—Mike Roberts, Franklin Pierce High School

Do your best, don't sweat the rest, and winning will take care of itself.
—Jim Wacker and Tom Mueller, Texas Christian University, and Sid Otton, Tumwater High School

Success is peace of mind, which is a direct result of self-satisfaction in knowing you made the effort to do your very best to become the best you are capable of becoming.
—John Wooden, University of California, Los Angeles

They remember November.
—R. C. Slocum, Texas A & M University

The games to remember are played in November.
—Tyler Hjelseth, Life Christian Academy

Success is a journey, not a destination.
—John Mackovic, University of Texas

It is not where you start that matters; it's where you finish.
—John Mackovic, University of Texas

He who shall, so shall he.
—Jim Christopherson, Concordia University, Minnesota

Be above average every day. It accumulates.
—Pat Simmers, North Dakota State University

Every defensive player must have three tools of the trade to be successful. A carpenter has a hammer, saw, etc. A mechanic has wrenches, gauges, sockets, etc. A good defensive player must be able to take on a block, get off a block, and make a tackle.
—Leo Ringey, North Dakota State University, and Larry Marmie, Arizona State University

Win the turnover battle. Win special teams. I love you guys. Have fun.
—Aron Kaye, Godinez Fundamental High School

The team that hits the hardest the longest will win.
—Buck Nystrom, Michigan State University

Give it your best shot.
—Frosty Westering, Pacific Lutheran University

Decide right now that you're going to do whatever it takes to be successful.
—Luke Balash, North Pole High School

Nothing grows on the mountaintops. Everything grows in the valleys.
—Bob Lucey, Curtis High School

I firmly believe that any man's finest hour, his greatest fulfillment of all he holds dear, is that moment when he has worked his heart out for a good cause and lies on the field of battle—victorious.
—Vince Lombardi, Green Bay Packers

It seems to me that more games are lost than won.
—John Wooden, University of California, Los Angeles

Win with three items: fundamentals, character, and loving one another.
—Lou Holtz, University of Notre Dame

The great teams because of pride, coaching, and loyalty are never broken, even in losing efforts.
—Ara Parseghian, University of Notre Dame

QUESTIONS TO AFFECT YOUR LIFE

1) With what part of Pat Lynn's story of recovery from adversity to success can you best identify?

2) Define *success* from your perspective. Have you achieved it?

3) What goal would you love to accomplish that you have not yet?

4) Why do some parents do better at putting their children on a path to success?

CHARACTER / INTEGRITY / LEGACY

Character

- The mental and moral qualities distinctive to an individual
- The particular combination of qualities in a person or place that makes them different from others[40]
- The quality of being determined and able to deal with difficult situations[41]
- Synonyms: personality, nature, psyche, makeup, temperament, constitution

Integrity

- The quality of being honest and having strong moral principles
- Synonyms: honesty, uprightness, virtue, honor, good character, principle, ethics, morals, morality, noble-mindedness, decency, fairness, fairness, scrupulousness, sincerity, truthfulness, trustworthiness

Legacy

- Something handed down or received from an ancestor or predecessor[42]
- Something ... that exists as a result of something that happened in the past; something that someone has achieved that continues to exist after they stop working or die[43]

- Synonyms: inheritance, heritage, endowment, benefaction; consequence, effect, outcome, footprint, result; fruits

THE CYCLE OF LIFE

In this final chapter, I offer perspective and insight into what I call the "cycle of life." When the idea of writing this book first came to mind, I saw it as a tool for influencing readers. My goal is to positively influence those who read this book so that they will, in turn, positively influence other people. This perpetuates the cycle of life, as learners who share their knowledge extend learning and influence to others.

Most people have at least a three-generation cycle of life and influence. For me, this included my parents from the Greatest Generation, my own baby boomer generation, and my sons from the millennial generation. Now I have entered a fourth generation of influence with my grandchildren. My cycle of life, like many of yours, began with learning from my parents. I grew through my young adult years to eventual maturity, and then I taught and influenced my sons, their peers, and now their spouses and children.

As we grow within our cycle of life, we have thousands of choices to make. Toward what outcomes do we make those choices? Why, for whom, and for what purpose? Whom do we choose to follow or emulate? When we need an inspiring word, to whom do we go?

As I reflect on each of the chapters in this book, it's clear to me that my intent is to extend my cycle of life influence to you and others. For what purpose? To help you and those you influence grow in becoming a better person, a better family, a better team, better employees, and better leaders. Each chapter topic was chosen for its key role in the cycle of life, and the people who contributed sayings are people who have influence. They, too, have been instrumental in helping shape rising generations.

As a husband, father, coach, educator, head of school, community leader, and now "Papa" to my grandchildren, my goal is simple: I want to use my life and influence to make other people's lives better in any way possible. For me, the words *character, integrity,* and *legacy* are central to the influence I want my cycle of life to have.

CHARACTER

Let me begin with my own early journey as a high school and college student. Each day, I was learning and developing who I was. My mother used to emphasize to me the importance of choosing my friends wisely. Why? Because of the influence they would have on me in the time we spent together. Though I didn't realize it at the time, my mother was conscious of and speaking into the development of my character and what it would mean to other people in the future. She was wise enough to have learned from other people's influence on her, and she was committed to helping me develop character that would cause me to influence people positively.

The definitions of character at the beginning of this chapter relate to a person's development. Character is continually being developed in all of us each day. My character is the sum total of the influence of other people on me, my own choices, and exercising the discipline to make the best decisions today to facilitate a better tomorrow. It is my hope that this book inspires you as you continue to develop your own character.

Who is the very best you? If you are like me, the best you is still under construction! Whether you're reading this at fifteen, thirty-five, sixty, or eighty, as long as you are taking in oxygen and nutrients, I believe you are still shaping your character. Character is developed over time, one decision at a time. Your decisions today determine your tomorrow.

What are we all looking for in our connections and relationships with other people? I think we all want people around us who will affect us positively. We all want good character to influence us. Coaches and leaders who "speak life" to others do so to encourage the development of great character in the next generation. We know that those with whom we have influence need positive deposits of solid character development, including words, actions, and prayers. Who says, "Oh, I have all the positive influence I need"? No one, because we all know that character is continuously under construction. Each day, for better or worse, we are developing our own character and influencing the character of others. It is up to us whether our influence is positive or negative.

Faith, discipline, training, relationships, leadership, and perseverance are all parts of character development. If you think back on your life, would you agree that your character today is the collective outcome of each of those influences? The same is true in helping to develop the character of other people. Character is who you are to others each day. What positive or negative influence do you have on your family, friends, colleagues at work, or others along your path? Your character is that influence. Do people get better when they are with you? Does your character cause others to improve?

Let me illustrate with a personal commendation. As mentioned in an earlier chapter, my best friend is Jerry Korum, a man I met at a men's Bible study in 1986. To this day I feel like I get better simply by spending time with Jerry. His character makes me better. What do I get from Jerry? I get a listening ear, compassion, wisdom, encouragement, timely advice, and a constant reliable source of good influence. At the end of our time together, I often say to him, "I get better every time I'm with you!" Thank you, Jerry.

INTEGRITY

One key aspect of character is integrity. Today's culture yearns for integrity in people. We all want to know and be connected to people we can trust—people who are honest, consistently dependable, and truthful every day. Integrity is consistent, visible, and influential, and it becomes even more apparent in the midst of chaos and failure. Proverbs 10:9 says, "The man of integrity walks securely, but he who takes crooked paths will be found out."

We appreciate people of integrity for who they are and who they can be counted on to be. A lack or failure of integrity often carries with it a high cost. As leaders rise within their organizations, their integrity or lack thereof is increasingly on display. Think of how many people you know whose lack of integrity has cost them significantly. Conversely, who continues to be an example of integrity in your life? Who provides you with that trustworthy, honest, and consistent influence each day?

My friend and pastor Wayde Goodall wrote a book titled *Why Great Men Fall: 15 Winning Strategies to Rise Above It All*. His book includes a chapter on integrity, which offers the following life principles to consider:

1. You're never wrong doing the right thing.
2. Do what you say you will do.
3. You are responsible for your life.
4. Respect people in general.
5. Give yourself an exam. How do you score?
6. Write out your rules of integrity and communicate them to those around you.
7. Stay on top of your game.

He also includes within the same chapter a reference from former president John F. Kennedy about our role as citizens and the President's belief that we will be measured by the answers to these four questions:

Were we men of courage?
Were we truly men of judgment?
Were we truly men of integrity?
Were we truly men of dedication?

Wayde also says that people can best evaluate themselves by examining the heart, and he offers four questions for consideration:

1. Do I have integrity in my heart?
2. Do I cut corners (cheat) in any area?

3. Do I justify my compromise (sin)?
4. Do I tolerate others who lack integrity?[44]

Thank you, Wayde, for your insights and your legacy.

Frosty Westering, longtime head coach at Pacific Lutheran University and one of the all-time winningest coaches in college football, frequently quoted a poem by Dale Wimbrow titled "The Guy in the Glass."

> When you get what you want in your struggle for pelf,
> And the world makes you King for a day,
> Then go to the mirror and look at yourself,
> And see what that guy has to say.
>
> For it isn't your Father, or Mother, or Wife,
> Who judgement upon you must pass.
> The feller whose verdict counts most in your life
> Is the guy staring back from the glass.
>
> He's the feller to please, never mind all the rest,
> For he's with you clear up to the end,
> And you've passed your most dangerous, difficult test
> If the guy in the glass is your friend.
>
> You may be like Jack Horner and "chisel" a plum,
> And think you're a wonderful guy,
> But the man in the glass says you're only a bum
> If you can't look him straight in the eye.
>
> You can fool the whole world down the pathway of years,
> And get pats on the back as you pass,
> But your final reward will be heartaches and tears
> If you've cheated the guy in the glass.[45]

LEGACY

In addition to character and integrity, another life-defining word is *legacy*. What is my legacy as a person? What is your legacy? Whose legacy do you learn from? Whose legacy has provided the most influence on your life thus far?

One dictionary defines *legacy* as "something handed down or received." When I personalize this definition, what is it that I want to hand down or others to inherit from me? A life lived with intention has daily opportunities to leave a legacy, a lasting influence.

Dr. Fulton Buntain served as senior pastor at Life Center in Tacoma, Washington, for forty-one years. One of his trademarks was a series of brief sayings—he called them "chin lifters"—that he frequently used to inspire and encourage his congregation and his friends. I used some of these sayings in the chapter on relationships. Here are a few of Pastor Buntain's chin lifters:

> It's always too soon to quit!
> God's power is always bigger than my problem.
> The only time you fail is the last time you try.
> The more you give thanks, the more you have to be thankful for.
> Things you appreciate tend to get better. Things you depreciate tend to get worse.
> If the wind doesn't blow, row!
> The difference between what I am and what I want to be is what I do.
> You can't change yesterday.

Pastor Buntain's substantial legacy includes numerous people like myself, who were influenced by not only his sermons but also his personal touch on people's lives. Life Center was a gathering place for thousands each weekend, yet most of them felt they knew their pastor personally. What a legacy he left in the lives of so many.

My personal mission statement, developed many years ago, is "to serve God and people to the best of my ability." This simple statement shapes my daily to-do list as well as my long-term aspirations and goals. As I live out this mission, my life should be creating a legacy that benefits people now, but that will also have a positive effect on their futures and the futures of yet others who may never even meet me.

In May 2019, I transitioned out of the headmaster role at Life Christian Academy after twenty-six years. I was blessed during this time to have been part of what the school has become. What LCA is today, and the education experiences it has provided to thousands of students and families, are the result of the efforts of hundreds of people. I was simply their leader.

At an event in my honor, fourteen people spoke to a crowd of friends, family, and colleagues gathered for a meal and celebration. After a few speakers had come and gone from the podium, it became obvious that the shared thread of their remarks was my legacy as a person, colleague, coach, and headmaster. Many people spoke of the effect of my leadership and the legacy I have left the school and the people it serves. Received with gratitude and humility, that evening provided me with a rich anecdote of my influence and legacy thus far.

Several years ago, I read *The Character of Leadership: An Ancient Model for a Quantum Age,* written by Philip Eastman II. His final chapter, "Developing a Leadership Legacy," includes this statement: "A leader has a unique and compelling reason to craft a legacy."[46]

In response to Eastman's urging to craft a legacy, I will use the remainder of this chapter to weigh in on what I hope my legacy is to people I have influenced over time. Like the many coaches and leaders quoted throughout these pages, I too, have used several sayings that my players, colleagues, and others automatically associate with me. Each comes from my life's learnings and strongest beliefs. Here's a sample:

> We get better or worse every day. We never stay the same.
> Enthusiasm is common. Endurance is rare.
> Shepherd the flock. These are my people and I am responsible for leading them.

Your tomorrow is the result of today's choices.
Life is half effort and half perseverance. You need both halves!
Prepare for the worst, but expect the best.
God bless America!

As a leader, it has been my journey to continually learn from others. Sometimes this learning has come from my own initiative to reach out, attend seminars, read, and listen to other leaders. Sometimes profound learning has come in the form of critique from others. Every time I met with parents of students in my role as coach or head of school, I was presented with an opportunity to listen and learn. I have found that more is learned by listening than by speaking. Seldom did I complete a meeting with parents without realizing I had learned from their perspective and insight. It is important that I learn from others, as I believe God teaches us through people He places in our lives.

My learnings have also come from influential people. Throughout my own legacy, I see the effect of others on my life, whether one of my first coaches, a best friend, or a colleague. I am thankful for these influences.

My friend Ben Newman wrote a chapter titled "Inspiring Legacy and Greatness in Others" in his book *Leave Your Legacy: The Power to Unleash Your Greatness.* In that chapter he included this quotation from Naveen Jain:

> I believe our legacy will be defined by the accomplishments and fearless nature by which our daughters and sons take on the global challenges we face. I also wonder if perhaps the most lasting expression of one's humility lies in the ability to foster and mentor our children.[47]

What will the next generation do with their lives, and to what degree will their accomplishments reflect my legacy? I believe any of us can ask this simple question, and the answers will come over time. The more intentionally we choose our actions based on the positive effect we want to have on the future, the more significant our legacy is likely to be.

I am thankful for the words that have been spoken over me and to me during my lifetime, and I have been intentional about collecting influential words from many throughout those years. This book has become, for me, a celebration of a life well lived because of influence, encouragement, and the blessings of God—creating a legacy, and helping you create yours.

To God be the glory!

SAYINGS

Character—true character—is what you are when no one is looking.
—Ken Rucker, University of Texas

Have some character, son. Don't be one.
—Bobby Hauck, University of Montana

Do right.
—Scott Smith, Legacy Christian Academy

You cannot soar with the eagles if you hang with the turkeys.
—Bob Lucey, Curtis High School

There is no right way to do the wrong thing!
—Numerous sources

It's not what you say in life that matters; it's what you do.
—Rich Brooks, University of Oregon

A man's birthright is his opportunity. His legacy is what he did with the opportunity.
—Ross Hjelseth

QUESTIONS TO AFFECT YOUR LIFE

1) What person or event has had the most significant influence on your character development?

2) What areas of your life do you find to be a negative influence on your integrity?

3) Whose legacy do you find yourself most trying to model or emulate? Why?

4) In a paragraph, take the time to describe the legacy you want to leave for other people.

NOTES

1   Chaim Ferster, *BBC News* (February 7, 2017).
2   "The Game Guy's Prayer," *Association Men*, vol. 46 (New York: International Committee of Young Men's Christian Associations, April 1921).
3   "The Gospel According to You," *The American Stationer*, vol. 74 (New York and Chicago, November 1913).
4   divineculbengan, "Training," BSBA Marketing, New Era University, Course Hero, 2019, coursehero.com/file/15159067/Training/.
5   *Macmillan Dictionary*, "to teach someone something: train," Springer Nature Limited, 2009–2019, macmillandictionary.com/us/thesaurus-category/american/to-teach-someone-something.
6   *BusinessDictionary*, s.v. "training," accessed 2019, businessdictionary.com.
7   *Merriam-Webster*, s.v. "training," accessed 2019, merriam-webster.com.
8   *Dictionary.com*, s.v. "train," accessed 2019, dictionary.com.
9   *Dictionary.com*, s.v. "training," accessed 2019, dictionary.com.
10 Syed Bahlki, "Self-Discipline Is a Foundation for Success" (March 11, 2014), https://syedbalkhi.com/selfdiscipline-foundation-success/.
11 "The Motto That Counts." James Whitcomb Riley, Electrical Merchandising, December 1919
12 *Dictionary.com*, s.v. "motivation," accessed 2019, dictionary.com.
13 Terry Liskevych and Todd Thorsteinson, "The Coach as Behavioral Engineer," *USVBA Level I Technical Module* (Los Angeles: Volleyball Association Publications, 1977).
14 Grant Teaff, "A Coach's Influence."
15 *Merriam-Webster*, s.v. "perseverance," accessed 2019, merriam-webster.com.
16 *Dictionary.com*, s.v. "perseverance," accessed 2019, dictionary.com.
17 Angela Duckworth, "Grit," article by Andrea Downing Peck, *Costco Connection* (Sept. 2018), pp. 44–49.

18   James Frederick Lawton, "When the Pressure's On." *Roses that Bloomed in the Snow: and Selected Poems*, University of Michigan "M" Club (Ann Arbor, MI: 1959).

19   "What is Leadership?" accessed 2019, mindtools.com/pages/article/newLDR_41.htm.

20   Sarmad Hasan, "Top 10 Leadership Qualities That Make Good Leaders," *TaskQue* (Feb. 13, 2017), blog.taskque.com/characteristics-good-leaders/.

21   Simon Sinek, *Start with Why* (Penguin, 2009).

22   Jonathan Franklin, "Luis Urzúa, the Foreman Keeping Hope Alive for Chile's Trapped Miners," *The Guardian* (Sept. 4, 2010), theguardian.com/world/2010/sep/05/luis-urzua-chile-trapped-miners.   Rory Carroll and Jonathan Franklin, "Chile Miners: Rescued Foreman Luis Urzúa's First Interview," *The Guardian* (Oct. 14, 2010), theguardian.com/world/2010/oct/14/chile-miner-luis-urzua-interview.

23   Stephen E. Ambrose, *Eisenhower: Soldier and President* (Simon and Schuster, 2014).

24   Theodore Roosevelt, "Citizenship in a Republic," Speech at the Sorbonne, Paris (April 23, 1910), leadershipnow.com/tr-citizenship.html.

25   This phrase has been frequently attributed to both Thomas Paine and George S. Patton, but no evidence exists of the authorship of either.

26   *Dictionary.com*, s.v. "relationship," accessed 2019, dictionary.com.

27   *Wikipedia,* s.v. "Interpersonal relationship," accessed Oct. 25, 2019, https://en.wikipedia.org/wiki/Interpersonal_relationship.

28   *Merriam-Webster,* s.v. "relationship," accessed 2019, merriam-webster.com.

29   Learn more about Ben's teaching and resources at www.bennewman.net.

30   Jerry Korum, "A–Z of Success in Life," jerry@korum.com.

31   *Wikipedia,* s.v. "teamwork," accessed Nov. 13, 2019, https://en.wikipedia.org/wiki/Teamwork.

32   *Wikipedia,* s.v. "team," accessed Nov. 15, 2019, https://en.wikipedia.org/wiki/Team.

33   Leigh Thompson, *Making the Team: A Guide for Managers*, 3rd ed. (Pearson/Prentice Hall, 2008).

34   *BusinessDictionary,* s.v. "team," accessed 2019, businessdictionary.com.

35   *Merriam-Webster Learner's Dictionary*, s.v. "success," accessed 2019, learnersdictionary.com.

36   *Merriam-Webster*, s.v. "success," Kids Definition of Success, accessed 2019, merriam-webster.com.

37   *BusinessDictionary,* s.v. "success," accessed 2019, businessdictionary.com.

38 Dale Carnegie, "Introduction," *How to Win Friends and Influence People* (Simon and Schuster, 1936).

39 Walter D. Wintle, "Thinking," *Unity Tract Society* (Unity School of Christianity, 1905).

40 *Cambridge English Dictionary*, s.v. "character," accessed 2019, dictionary. cambridge.org.

41 *Cambridge English Dictionary*, s.v. "character," accessed 2019, dictionary. cambridge.org.

42 *Collins English Dictionary*, s.v. "legacy," accessed 2019, collinsdictionary.com.

43 *Macmillan Dictionary*, s.v. "legacy," Springer Nature Limited, 2009–2019, macmillandictionary.

44 Wayde Goodall, *Why Great Men Fall* (New Leaf, 2005).

45 Dale Wimbrow, "The Guy in the Glass," *American Magazine* (May 1934), theguyintheglass.com/gig.htm.

46 Phillip H. Eastman II, *The Character of Leadership* (Leadership Advisors, 2009).

47 Ben Newman, "Inspiring Greatness and Legacy in Others," *Leave YOUR Legacy* (Greenleaf Book Group, 2015).